THE
SUCCESS
PROFILE

A LEADING HEADHUNTER TELLS YOU HOW TO GET TO THE TOP

LESTER KORN

SIMON AND SCHUSTER

NEW YORK   LONDON   TORONTO   SYDNEY   TOKYO

Published by Simon and Schuster
A Division of Simon & Schuster Inc.
Simon & Schuster Building
Rockefeller Center
1230 Avenue of the Americas
New York, New York 10020
SIMON AND SCHUSTER and colophon are registered trademarks
of Simon & Schuster Inc.

Designed by Irving Perkins Associates
Manufactured in the United States of America

10 9 8 7 6 5 4 3 2 1

Library of Congress Cataloging in Publication Data

Korn, Lester.
  The Success Profile.

  1. Executive ability. 2. Executives—Recruiting.
3. Chief executive officers—Recruiting. 4. Success
in business. 5. Corporate culture. I. Title.
HD38.2.K67   1988   658.4'09   87-23249

ISBN 0-671-55263-5

ACKNOWLEDGMENTS

There are many people to whom I am grateful for helping me make *The Success Profile* a reality.

First and foremost, I thank my friend and editor Michael Korda, editor-in-chief of Simon and Schuster. Michael insisted throughout that I continue with this book, even when I offered to return my generous advance on more than one occasion. His belief in the book was a continuing source of inspiration; his editing witty, pungent, and always correct; his availability immediate, even when it was by telephone from Africa. His insights, care, and advice helped me to understand why he is generally acknowledged to be the leading editor of our times. I shall never forget his generous encouragement and his commitment to this project.

My co-writer, Ed Zuckerman, was a constant pleasure to work with and contributed invaluably with his cheerfulness and professionalism.

My partners at Korn/Ferry International encouraged the book, reviewed sections of it, and made many useful suggestions. I am particularly grateful to Lucie Adam, whose probing questions and continuous review and encouragement kept this project going. Her help was immeasurable.

A very special note of appreciation to my friends and colleagues at Josephson International and the ICM talent-agency group, whose board I have served on for many years. My friend Marvin Josephson, to whom I turned immediately when I was asked to write this book (I was sitting in the Concorde Lounge waiting for a London flight when the offer was made), watched over the project constantly. His approval, when it came, convinced me that I had achieved my objective—to take readers into my world and help them help themselves.

I especially appreciate the efforts of Luis Sanjurjo, my late agent at ICM. I'm grateful that I had a chance to work with him

5

through most of the writing of the book, and I wish he had lived to see its publication. I shall miss his friendship, guidance, and constant good spirits.

Throughout this book, I rely on a historic study conducted by Korn/Ferry International and the John E. Anderson Graduate School of Management at UCLA. The study, "Korn/Ferry International's Executive Profile: A Survey of Corporate Leaders," was first conducted in 1979, again in 1984 and updated by the authors for this book. It has given the business world one of its few statistically reliable data bases on senior executives. The dedicated researchers at both Korn/Ferry International and UCLA, including J. Clayburn La Force, Dean of the Anderson School, have my deep appreciation. We all work less in darkness as a result of their studies.

Finally, I am extremely grateful to my friends and colleagues in the business world who gave so generously of their time and shared so many of their most private views and insights. Men and women of substantial accomplishment, they came from diverse backgrounds to achieve success. One theme runs through their stories: they planned their careers. My thanks to all of them:

Donald Beall, president, Rockwell International

Norman Blake, chairman, Heller International Corporation.

Richard Braddock, sector executive, Citicorp

Thornton Bradshaw, former president, Atlantic Richfield Company, and former chairman, RCA

John Chamberlin, president, Avon Products, Inc.

Raymond Dempsey, chairman, European American Bank

Roger Enrico, president, Pepsi-Cola Company

Jane Evans, general partner, Montgomery Securities

William Glavin, vice chairman, Xerox Corporation

Harry Gray, former chairman, United Technologies Corporation

Darryl Hartley-Leonard, president, Hyatt Hotels Corporation

James Harvey, chairman, Transamerica Corporation

Rita Hauser, senior partner, Stroock & Stroock & Lavan

Raymond A. Hay, chairman & CEO, LTV Corporation

Larry Horner, chairman, Peat Marwick Main & Co.

Jane Hurd, former CEO, Children's Hospital of Los Angeles

Frederic B. Malek, executive vice president, Marriott Corporation

Marshall Manley, president & CEO, The Home Group

Donald B. Marron, chairman & CEO, Paine Webber Group Inc.

Douglas H. McCorkindale, vice chairman, chief financial & administrative officer, Gannett Company

Paul M. Montrone, president, The Henley Group

Caroline W. Nahas, vice president, Korn/Ferry International

Philip L. Smith, vice chairman, Philip Morris Companies, Inc., and president and CEO, General Foods (recently appointed CEO of Pillsbury)

William D. Smithburg, chairman, The Quaker Oats Company

Albert R. Snider, executive vice president, operations, Avnet, Inc.

William H. Waltrip, former president, IU International Corp.

Gary L. Wilson, executive vice president, The Walt Disney Company

And, most importantly, a word of special appreciation to Richard M. Ferry, my partner, friend and co-founder of Korn/Ferry International, for his advice, friendship and encouragement in all things. It is my good fortune to be able to say I have yet to meet a finer person or a better executive.

With love to Carolbeth, Jodi, and Jessica

CONTENTS

PREFACE

AT FIRST glance, a book about how to succeed in the corporate world might seem intended only for those still making their ways up the corporate ladder. But if I have succeeded in what I set out to do, this book contains lessons and suggestions for executives at every level, including the very top.

These lessons come not only from my own experience but also from that of the two dozen chief executives who consented to be interviewed for this book. Their candid recollections constitute a case-study course in corporate careers.

The most striking thing about the executives' stories is how many elements they share. In my work with chief executive officers, I have encountered many who are proud of how they marshaled their own intelligence and tenacity to reach the top; they suspect, on the other hand, that many of their peers in other companies had an easier time of it. In fact, nobody has an easy time getting to the top. Everybody struggles at critical points in his or her career. Every chief executive we interviewed had to make sacrifices, had to overcome blocks, had to take chances, had to plan thoughtfully, and had to deliberately and methodically lay the groundwork for his or her own crucial "lucky" break. In their accounts of how they met these challenges lie the lessons of this book.

For chief executives who want to compare war stories, there are plenty here. For junior executives who think they are facing problems unique to their own offices (or bosses' personalities), there will be solace in realizing that many of today's chief executive officers faced identical

15

problems years ago, and there will be edification in learning how they overcame them.

A different set of lessons may be drawn from this book by senior management. Today's young executives are more mobile and less loyal than executives of the past. They are, however, just as good, so there is reason to try to understand their goals and motivations. Satisfy them, and they *will* be loyal.

One of my recurrent themes is the importance of communication between subordinate and boss. I urge subordinates repeatedly to confront their bosses to find out how they stand. What does the company think of them? Are they considered promotable? Why are they earning what they earn? I believe all ambitious executives must learn these things, even if it means raising questions that most employees are too abashed to ask.

If they cannot get answers to these questions, then I advise them to get ready to change jobs. In many cases, this means their current employers will be losing good people. Often, such employers' reticence in telling junior people what they need to know to plan their careers proceeds not from any sound policy reason but simply from the fact that bosses are uncomfortable talking about such things. It behooves those at the top to root out such antiproductive reticence in their own companies. A wise chief executive will make an effort to understand what ambitious subordinates need to know about the progress of their careers—and then will open channels to make sure they get to know it.

Ultimately, by doing well for themselves, today's bright young executives will do good for the companies that employ them. Companies that provide them with the opportunities they seek will be amply rewarded by their productivity and competitiveness, as will the entire American economy. Amid today's international economic competition, we need to encourage the ambitious among us. I hope this book will help them succeed, and help their bosses help them as well.

PART I

THE SIX-FIGURE
EXECUTIVE

I'VE SEEN them come and I've seen them go.

As co-founder and chairman of the largest and most successful executive-recruiting firm in the world, I have spent almost two decades locating and placing top-level executives. I have seen thousands of promising men and women reach key breakpoints in their careers and proceed to make the right moves to propel themselves into senior management. It has been my pleasure to place those rising executives in their new positions.

I have also seen people stumble. Many of these people were just as bright and just as hardworking as those who succeeded, but they neglected to make the most of their assets and failed to position themselves properly for career ascent.

I could see what they did wrong, just as I saw what their successful peers did right. My two decades of experience with executive careers have given me the greatest education anyone could have in career development. Because of my reputation as a leading "headhunter," strangers often hand me their résumés when they recognize me in airports or offices, and they ask me for my help. This is somewhat inconvenient when I am running for a plane, so I am setting down here answers to the questions I am most frequently asked. The next time someone shoves a résumé at me and asks what I think, I will have something helpful to give back.

THE KILLING FIELDS

If you're between the ages of twenty-five and forty-one, you're a baby-boomer, and some pretty dire prognostications have been issued on the possibility of your advancing into the ranks of senior corporate management. You're supposedly part of a management glut, and you're condemned by the demographers to be fighting the mob for the rest of your career. The same bulge in the population that created such a terrific market for personal computers, condominiums, designer clothes, and Lean Cuisine has supposedly clogged the corridors of power.

Following this reasoning, if you're over forty or in your mid-twenties, you're not much better off. Members of the older generation have the ambitious, hard-charging baby-boomers breathing down their necks, and the younger people will always be standing in line behind the baby-boomers, waiting for them to retire sometime in the twenty-first century.

Now, there is some truth in all of this. Competition is intense for good jobs today; the baby boom and the educational free-for-all of the past few decades have given corporate America the largest and best-trained manpower pool in history. Compounding the problem is the fact that entry-level and middle-management positions were heavily pruned during the recession of the early 1980s. Since 1979, the Bureau of Labor Statistics estimates, more than half a million managerial positions have been eliminated at the nation's leading companies. Some were lost to recession, others to corporate mergers, acquisitions, and divestitures. Many of those jobs are gone for good. Company after company has found virtue in necessity and is bragging about maintaining its new "lean and mean" management structure.

At the same time that the mid-level positions which provide a transition platform to top management were being cut back, a new generation was coming of age with fiercely competitive attitudes. Whatever remains of the 1960s antibusiness ethos has disappeared almost entirely from the nation's campuses. Today's generation wants to succeed; it has no qualms about succeeding; and it refuses to accept the "limits to growth" philosophy. "More is beautiful" has become the dominant theme of American life.

Fortunately, the turmoil on the business scene in recent years has been accompanied by opportunity. As old industries wither, new industries arise. New products replace those which have run their course. There has already been much talk about the growth of high-technology and service industries. In our search work, we see opportunities just as great in the creative repositioning of old industries. To name just one, health care was once a sleepy, nonprofit area; today it is booming. Health-care companies are looking for more managers with business expertise than they can find. Elsewhere, new growth is appearing in previously unimagined areas. Retail stores have become brokerage offices; brokerage houses have become banks; prison administration has become a business, as has the conversion of garbage to electricity. Even the old "rust belt" industries offer fabulous opportunities for creative managers with the imagination and initiative to introduce more efficient manufacturing processes and innovative new products based on the latest technological advances.

Most important, it is ridiculous to assume that America has finished growing. Our history is replete with warnings of limited career opportunity. Over the long term, those warnings have never been correct. There always have been, and there always will be, plenty of opportunities for those who would seize them.

If you fail to reach the top, the fault will not be with the state of the economy, or the prime rate, or Toyota; it will be with yourself. You will get good jobs if you make yourself the best possible candidate for those jobs. Not

everybody can reach the top, but *somebody has to*. Even
the demographers would agree with that.

THE EDUCATION OF A HEADHUNTER

My company, Korn/Ferry International, started small.
Dick Ferry and I started it up in 1969, leaving good positions as young partners in the accounting firm of Peat
Marwick and Company for the uncertain future of young
entrepreneurs. I had done executive-search work for Peat
Marwick, and I had enjoyed it. I liked meeting with chief
executive officers and helping them work through their
thinking processes. I saw that these executives were eager
for help in evaluating people. It was something they were
not comfortable doing themselves. It didn't bother me; I
was happy to make judgments about the way people perform. My record of predicting success was turning out to
be excellent. And I could see that the unease management felt about the task pointed the way to a rosy future
for the executive-search business.

Our future did turn out to be rosy, but our success was
by no means assured when we set out. At the ages of
thirty-two and thirty-three, respectively, Dick and I were
retiring from the world's largest accounting firm. (In
those days, there was no provision for a partner's resign-
ing. It was unheard of for partners to resign. They either
retired or died.) We worried that we would starve together
in our brave new venture. But we set off nonetheless. We
were about to call our firm Korn/Ferry Associates when a
friend (Milan Panic, chairman of ICN Pharmaceuticals)
advised us not to think small. "Call it Korn/Ferry International," he said. "You're going to be international someday, aren't you?"

So, as Korn/Ferry International, we opened offices in
Los Angeles and New York. We also had, by a fluke, an
office in San Marino, a Los Angeles suburb. We had not
been sure we could use our own names in the firm because of our contractual obligations to Peat Marwick, so
we had purchased a moribund San Marino executive-
search firm, with plans to adopt its name if necessary. In
the end, we were able to use our own, but we were left
with the office in San Marino. Everybody assumed that
was in Europe, justifying our international title, even
though our "European" office was exactly fourteen miles
from our headquarters in Los Angeles.

Today, I am proud to say that Korn/Ferry International
is the largest executive-search firm in the world. We have
thirty-seven offices in sixteen countries (but not San
Marino). We have placed thousands of people in management jobs, the vast majority at senior levels. In 1986
alone we conducted searches for 1,780 people in jobs paying salaries totaling well over $200 million.

We have recruited executives for IBM, Merrill Lynch,
Citicorp, General Electric, Shearson Lehman, Morgan
Grenfell, Walt Disney, Yamaha Motors, Barclays Bank,
Nissan Motors, and hundreds of other major corporations
in the United States and around the world. We have recruited managers for the Reagan White House, the Ford
and Rockefeller foundations, and entities of the government of Mexico. We have undertaken assignments to find
a U.S. Postmaster General, a president of Monaco's business interests for Prince Rainier, a president for the Fed-
eral National Mortgage Association ("Fannie Mae"), and
cabinet ministers for the governments of Belgium and
Great Britain.

Among the chief executive officers we have placed are
Raymond Dempsey of European American Bank, Marvin
Runyon of Nissan USA, Charles Lynch of DHL World-
wide Express, and Ryal Poppa of Storage Technology. We
have also recruited the director of the San Francisco Museum of Modern Art and the city manager of Dallas.

In 1985, Peter Ueberroth became the first *Time* magazine "Man of the Year" to win the honor for his perfor-

mance in a job for which he had been recruited by an executive-search firm. It was Korn/Ferry International, working for the Los Angeles Olympic Organizing Committee, that found Ueberroth for the job of running the phenomenally successful 1984 Games. (And a reluctant candidate he was, saying "no" many times before the challenge of the "no-win" opportunity proved too much for him to pass up. His case proved for the millionth time that executive recruiters have to be persistent.)

Every placement we have made has been another step in my own education. Every time we conduct a search, we consider dozens of candidates for the position. We pore over résumés like scholars and have learned to cull the exceptional from the merely good. Often the résumés tell sad stories—of talented executives who have made bad decisions and squandered their promise by getting themselves trapped in dead-end career paths. Sometimes it is because they failed to move when they should have; sometimes it is because they have moved too much.

When I encounter such careers, I want to leap in and tell those involved what they are doing wrong. Often it is not too late to make a saving change—if only they knew that they were on the wrong path.

THE WORLD'S BEST ADVICE

Reading this book can help you rise in the corporate world—and not just because of what *I* know. Two dozen chief executive officers, chief operating officers, and chief financial officers of major American companies consented to tell their stories for this book. Among them are some of the best-known names in American business— Harry Gray of United Technologies, Roger Enrico of Pepsi-Cola, Donald Marron of Paine Webber, Marshall

Manley of The Home Group, Donald Beall of Rockwell, Larry Horner of KPMG Peat Marwick, James Harvey of Transamerica. Many of these men and women have over the years generally avoided speaking to the press. Through this book, for the first time (and with my very deep gratitude), they tell the stories of their careers—where they took their first jobs, and why; when they switched jobs, and why; when they fought with their bosses, and why; how they maneuvered their way around career blocks; when they did nothing, and why; how they got to the top.

To expand our data base on executive career planning, Korn/Ferry International has conducted, in conjunction with the UCLA Graduate School of Management, one of the most extensive surveys ever taken of senior-level executives. More than 1,300 senior executives (up to but excluding CEOs and COOs) of the largest corporations in America (all are on the Fortune 500 list of industrial or service companies) responded to detailed questionnaires about their jobs, attitudes, personal backgrounds, and career histories. These executives, whose average annual compensation is $235,000, have provided us with a remarkable mosaic of life at the top of American business—and of the road to the top. Throughout this book, I will dip into the results of that survey to develop the lessons they teach.

One unique aspect of the survey was a retroactive salary history. Each respondent was asked to report what his or her salary was at five-year intervals from age twenty-five to the present. By adjusting the answers for inflation, our research analysts have produced the first-ever constant-dollar executive age/wage ratio that I consider reliable. We have computed—by industry, by managerial specialty, by number of job changes, and overall—a lifetime age/wage yardstick of success based on the histories of our respondents. Our findings provide truly useful information, as the first step in moving ahead is learning what you could be worth on the job market. You may enjoy measuring your own income against the standard our survey respondents have set, or it may depress you. In any case, it makes very clear that the old rule of thumb "earn your age" ($1,000 for every year) is now of only historical interest..

THE SIX-FIGURE-EXECUTIVE PROFILE

Who are today's six-figure executives? How did they get there? What do they believe? From our survey results and our experience, we can paint a picture of the typical senior executive:

Table 1–1

PROFILE OF SENIOR EXECUTIVES

Average age.. 51
Average salary.................................... $235,000
Definition of success............................enjoyment of work
Reason for success.............................. hard work
Average hours per work week..................... 56
Days spent away on business.....................49/year
Average number of vacation days..................14/year
Considered the fastest route to the top........... marketing
Considered the fastest route 10 years from now... marketing
Number who aspire to be CEO..................... 49%
Percentage of women executives.................. 2%
Percentage of minority executives................ 1%
Education....................................... BS/MBA
Percentage of married executives.................94%
Executives with working wives................... 29%
Politics.. 74% Republican
Religion.. 58% Protestant

Highlights from "The Korn/Ferry International Executive Profile: A Survey of Corporate Leaders in the Eighties"

Table 1–2

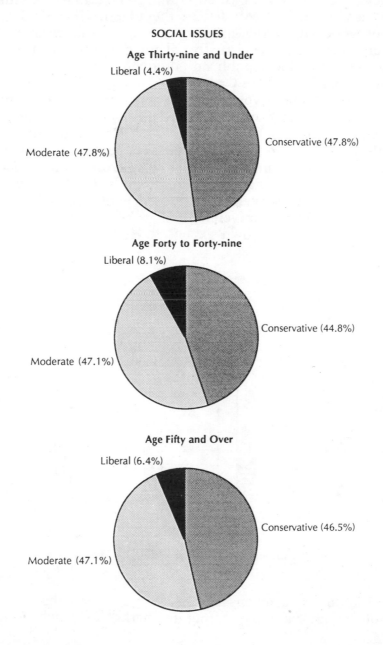

SOCIAL ISSUES

Age Thirty-nine and Under

Liberal (4.4%)

Moderate (47.8%)

Conservative (47.8%)

Age Forty to Forty-nine

Liberal (8.1%)

Moderate (47.1%)

Conservative (44.8%)

Age Fifty and Over

Liberal (6.4%)

Moderate (47.1%)

Conservative (46.5%)

He is fifty-one years old, white, male, married (and never divorced) with three children. (A handful of his peers are female; I will discuss them later.) His wife does not work outside the home (neither did his mother). His corporate peers are virtually all male and white. He is Protestant and a Republican (although a substantial minority of his peers are Catholic and a handful are Jewish). He almost always votes, and he considers himself to be conservative on fiscal issues and moderate to conservative on social issues (see Table 1–2). He doesn't smoke (although he once may have). He says he drinks "moderately"; he has some colleagues who drink "often." He grew up in a "normal" two-parent family. His father was a white-collar worker. He attended public schools and probably a public university, where he earned a significant portion of his own expenses. He has an MBA (see Table 1–3).

Table 1–3

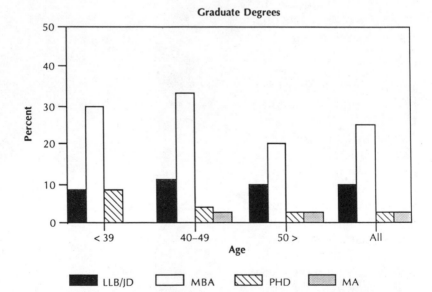

His annual compensation is $235,000, and that does not include the many corporate "perks" to which he is entitled. He first broke the $100,000-a-year-barrier (in 1987 dollars) at or before the age of thirty-five, as a vice president.

This remarkable early financial breakthrough went hand in hand with what he considers to be the major turning point in his career, which occurred, on average, at age thirty-four. He attributes that breakthrough to timing —being in the right place at the right time—and to having made a move to a different functional responsibility. (He began his career in finance or accounting. Many of his peers started in marketing or a professional or technical capacity. Now he works in general management.)

He says he believes that executive mobility is important and that an executive's chances for advancement are improved if he does *not* remain with the same company through his entire career. He himself, however, has worked for only two companies and has worked for his current employer for seventeen years. (Many of his younger colleagues, however, are changing jobs more often.) When he has changed employers, he has done so in pursuit of increased job responsibility and challenge, not money.

He believes that he has reached his level of success primarily through hard work, ambition, and luck; he firmly believes it is "what he knows," not "whom he knows," that has made him what he is. He thinks integrity is of paramount importance in a successful career. Concern for results and the desire for responsibility are also crucial.

He is satisfied with his job and would continue to work at it even if he were financially independent. If he were starting all over again, he would pursue the same or a similar career. On the other hand, he does not intend to work past age sixty-five.

He works fifty-six hours a week and takes only fourteen vacation days a year.

He aspires to be chief executive officer. He may make it. (And soon, I believe, so may *she*.)

DO YOU FIT THE BILL?

You cannot turn yourself into a WASP if you aren't one. If you're a woman, you can't become a man in time for a job interview next week. Many bright and capable people do not fit the demographic profile of the typical senior executive, and they never will.

Fortunately, they don't have to. Male WASPs still have an edge in the corporate world, but that edge is no longer a matter of institutional policy. Many companies have made major commitments, and are expending considerable effort, to hire women and blacks and others who do not fit the traditional corporate stereotype. It will take years for these newly hired people to work their way up the corporate pyramid (remember, the average age of our respondents is fifty-one), but they surely will. The inevitability of that progress, at least in the area of sex, was plainly illustrated in a brochure that recently crossed my desk. It came from Merrill Lynch's merger-and-acquisitions department, and it contained photographs of the entire staff. There were nine managing directors; all were male. There were seventeen vice presidents; all were male. There were ten associates; half were female. By the time you read this, some of those women will have become vice presidents.

Today, whether you are a white male or a black female, the corporate playing field is more level than it has ever been. The top spots are open to anyone who earns them. Executives who know how to produce positive results for their companies, *and know how to put themselves into positions where their work can be seen and appreciated*, will rise to senior ranks.

But no one will rise who does not work at it. Successful careers do not just happen. They are planned. Those who succeed in corporate life are those who take control of their own careers. They know where they want to go, and they take steps to get there. They constantly measure the progress of their careers against their plans, and the mere fact that they *have* plans sets them apart in a critical way from the peers they leave behind in the dust.

PLAN, PLAN, PLAN

I'm going to talk a great deal about planning in this book. Because if I know anything from my experience in dealing with thousands of executive careers, it is this:

You cannot reach the ranks of top management by blithely sitting at your desk every day and doing your job —even if you do it very, very well—and assuming that everything is going to work out fine.

You might reach the ranks of *middle* management that way. It's not really that hard to make $75,000 to $100,000 (approximately middle-management income) in corporate America nowadays. The money is good in corporate life. With just a little luck and even halfhearted planning, competence and longevity may carry you into the near-six-figure bracket.

If you're content to coast up to that middle level (or near it) and then dead-end, you may as well stop reading right now. Because this book is for those who want to reach the top and are willing to work at it. I don't mean working at their jobs. It's taken for granted that *everybody* is working at his or her job. I mean working at developing their careers. (And I mean doing so *ethically*. The sad sight of ambitious young people caught in the recent insider-trading scandals is a tragic waste. Fortunately for America, such unethical behavior is far from universal. It is also unnecessary for success.)

The first step in getting anywhere, of course, is knowing where it is you want to go. This should be so obvious that it doesn't need saying. But it does. I'm constantly amazed by the number of mid-level executives I encounter who have no precise idea of where they want to go,. except, vaguely, "up."

Lee Iacocca knew where he wanted to go. According to *Iacocca* (not the autobiography of the same name, but the biography by David Abodaher), Iacocca boasted to his college classmates that he would become a vice president of the Ford Motor Company before his thirty-fifth birthday. Seventeen years later, just thirteen months after his self-declared deadline, he achieved his goal.

Few executives know, or *can* know, exactly what they aspire to until they have been in the work force for a couple of years. It takes that long to learn enough about yourself to know what you can do well and what will make you happy. The trick then is to merge the two into a goal, then set off in pursuit of it.

At every stage in your unfolding career, as the following years go by, you must periodically stand outside yourself and cold-bloodedly look at where you are and determine if it is indeed on the path to where you want to be. It's easy to know that it's time for a change if you find yourself at an obvious dead end. But there are often trickier cases. You might have a very good job. It might be a high-paying job. It might clearly be the launching pad to an excellent career. But unless it is the launching pad to the career you are seeking, it is wrong for you, and you will have to make a change. This is a simple truth, but often a hard one to accept.

Making that change might involve leaving the company, or only changing jobs within the company. It might require that you move to another state or country, or only that you take a different attitude toward your current work. It might involve no change in your job at all but only that you take steps to make sure certain people are aware of what you're doing there.

It is easier, of course, not to spend a lot of time analyzing your career. You have enough to worry about just taking care of your *job*. And is anything extra really necessary? you wonder. You already have on your side, after all, intelligence, ambition, and a willingness to work hard.

Sure, but who doesn't, nowadays? Look around you. And when you do, take note of the older executives you see who are smarter than you (be honest, now), just as ambitious, and just as hardworking, who have not succeeded. What are they missing?

"You have to have a strategic sense," says Gary Wilson, who has followed a seemingly erratic but in fact brilliantly planned career path to the number-three job (executive vice president and chief financial officer) at the Walt Disney Company. "If you're going to be a senior executive, you have to have a strategic sense about your business, and you also have to have a strategic sense about yourself. So many times we get caught up in the day-to-day commotion of this deal and that deal, and will I get this promotion and that promotion, that we lose sight of the whole picture.... If you know what you're trying to accomplish, and just kind of outline it in rough form, it makes the probability of achieving it that much greater."

JOB VS. CAREER

One thing to keep in mind right from the beginning is the crucial distinction between your job and your career. Your job belongs to your employer. It is a specified function in a corporate matrix. If you don't do it, somebody else will. To reach your goals, you must do your job well. But do not get lost in your job. It is not an end in itself. It is a means to an end—your career.

Your career belongs to you. It is your plan, your dream, your *life*. You will have many jobs in the course of your career (even if you have only one employer). You will do each one of them well, but you will be looking beyond each one of them even as you are doing it. You will be calculating how it can lead you to the next job on your career ladder. When it serves its purpose, and gets you that better job, you will immediately look beyond the new job to what lies ahead from there.

Because you are not just seeking "a better job." You are seeking a successful career.

PART 2

PREREQUISITES FOR SUCCESS

W HY DO some people succeed while others do not? Some contributing factors are clear; others are muddy at best. Very few people wake up one morning at the age of thirty-five and suddenly set off for the top (although a few do). The roots of success seem to be planted much earlier. Some of them have to do with human nature. Certain personality traits are conducive to success; either people have them or they do not. But one's fate is not cast in stone. Fortunately for all of us, most important factors in the quest for success are the results of conscious decisions, deliberately arrived at. Anyone who takes the care to do so can give him- or herself a boost by making those decisions correctly. Finally, there is the matter of simple luck—only luck, as we shall see, is never a "simple" factor in the careers of the successful. If luck fails to find them, they go out and find it.

ARE YOU THE RIGHT KIND OF PERSON?

Those who succeed in corporate America tend to share certain traits of personality. These include:

ENERGY

You cannot play a responsible role in a major corporation if you have trouble getting out of bed before 9 A.M.. Corporate leaders tend to get up at 6 A.M.—and like it. They don't want to take a nap on Saturday afternoon. They want to *do* something. Do you?

LIKABILITY

Obnoxious people do succeed, but it is easier to succeed if you are a nice person. I don't mean a patsy; I mean someone who gets along with people, who respects them and is respected by them. If there are two equally accomplished candidates for a promotion, and one is well liked and one is not, who do you think is going to get the job?

INTELLIGENCE

According to an old law-school wheeze, A students become law professors, B students become judges—and C students become successful lawyers. This is a slight distortion of reality; you *do* have to be smart to succeed in business. There are no dummies sitting in the chief-executive offices of major corporations or other organizations (although there are some C students). But sheer intelligence must be balanced by practicality. And exceptional intelligence can be counterproductive; it may be perceived as threatening by those around you, and it may interfere with your own decision-making if it enables you to see a crippling number of alternative courses of action.

INTEGRITY

This was rated the most important factor in enhancing one's chances for success by our survey respondents, and I believe they are correct. It is disturbing, therefore, that so many young people today apparently believe otherwise. One of the executives we interviewed serves on the student-affairs committee of the board of trustees of his alma mater. "A student was caught plagiarizing a paper last year," he reports. "And the student court determined that he was guilty and suspended him from school. The student body went into an uproar, because this student already had a job offer and the suspension was screwing that up. The students' attitude knocked me off my chair. It was 'Everybody does it. That's the way business is. Don't worry about it.' I reported this to the board, and every guy in that room felt the same way I did, that this was terrible, that these people have a totally incorrect view of what business is all about."

DRIVE

This is *the* indispensable requirement for success: you have to want it, and want it badly. "You have to have a will to accomplish whatever it is you're setting out to accomplish," says Rita Hauser, who had to overcome formidable barriers of sex discrimination to become one of the leading female attorneys of her generation. "I believe in will. I think the will to succeed, the will to win, the will to overcome adversity is an absolute major force in the success of anybody."

THE WILLINGNESS TO SACRIFICE

Success does not come without a price, a price that those who rise to the heights of corporate America are prepared to pay.

Our survey shows that senior executives work an average of fifty-six hours a week, and they certainly did not work any less than that while they were on their way up. When they were asked to name the single most important factor in their own success, the most common answer by far was "hard work." (Ambition ranked second.)

I know from my own experience that people who succeed work when others do not. I frequently deal with chief executive officers, and I often find it convenient to telephone them on weekends. Invariably, they are happy to take my calls. Even though they're at home and it's Sunday, they're working. (At one point in his career at Litton Industries, Harry Gray, later the chairman of

United Technologies, held staff meetings at his home at
7 A.M. on Sundays. "It was a situation where we needed to
do a lot of work," he recalls. "We were working on Saturdays and then what we didn't finish up on Saturday we
did on Sunday morning, and then everybody could go to
church, and then the rest of the day was for family.")

These brutal hours are ameliorated by the fact that successful people *enjoy* working. They get satisfaction from
it that other people get from sports or hobbies. "When
you've seen one castle, you've seen them all," a promi-
nent businessman once said to explain why he had returned to work from a scheduled two-week European
vacation after a few days.

The greatest sacrifices successful business people face
are in the area of family life. Wallace Rasmussen, the
former chairman of Beatrice Foods, is reported by *Fortune*
to have told a meeting that "running a corporation is a
twenty-hour-a-day, seven-day-a-week job. 'What about
your wife and family?' one listener asked. 'Get rid of
them if they get in the way,' Rasmussen snapped."

That is, of course, an extreme attitude (and not one I
endorse). Many executives are scrupulous—and organized—about spending time with their families. "My son
gets up at five forty-five," says Darryl Hartley-Leonard,
president of Hyatt Hotels. "And I get up at five forty-five,
and we play for fifteen or twenty minutes. It is a schedule. At six fifteen, I get into the shower. By six forty-five, I
am walking out the front door. And by seven thirty, three
days a week, I am at a breakfast meeting. It has to be that
way."

Hartley-Leonard and others like him work hard to
make sure their families are not slighted, but many executive families do suffer. Families that stay together are
often forced to make sacrifices *en masse* when an executive is transferred to another city, which usually seems to
happen just when Junior has won a place on the school
soccer team.

There is an up side to this. Most of the successful executives I know have found happy balances in their lives.

And remember, if you work in the corporate world, you will be forced to make sacrifices even if you spend your entire career no higher than middle management. It's no harder to be at the top than it is to be in the middle, so you might as well be at the top.

ARE YOU *ALREADY* A SUCCESS?

One of the best predictors of whether you will have a successful corporate career is whether or not you are *already* a success. Success is a habit. A person who has achieved some success is likely to be self-confident, to understand how to work effectively, and to attract the interest of potential employers. If you are already doing well for your age, you are likely to continue to do so.

A look at the lives of successful executives shows a continuing pattern of achievement going back to their very early years. As a paperboy in Alliance, Ohio, Gary Wilson (now executive vice president of the Walt Disney Company) demonstrated his business acumen. "The local paper gave out routes," he recalls, "and you had the right to trade them. I started out with a very small route, and I ended up with the biggest paper route in town. When I got to high school, I hired somebody to do the routes for me, so I was really running my own business. I took the money I made and invested in my stamp collection, and it has turned out to be a very good investment over the years."

Larry Horner, the dynamic chairman of KPMG Peat Marwick, grew up in a small town in Kansas. When he was in high school, he scraped together the money to buy a combine. In the summers, he hired other youths and they traveled through the state as a free-lance harvesting crew. "By the time I graduated I probably had seven or eight combines," he says. He used his profits to buy land.

"By the time I graduated I probably had several hundred acres."

Such early successes exhibit not only business sense but such other essential traits as drive and energy. Fred Malek, who is today executive vice president of the Marriott Corporation, attended West Point. The first blossoming of his commercial instincts had to wait until after he had graduated and served six months with the Special Forces in Vietnam, where he trained Vietnamese ranger companies in counterguerrilla tactics. "We taught them how to set up an ambush, how to counter an ambush, how to raid a village. By raiding a village I don't mean going in and shooting everybody; I mean flushing out the Viet Cong and having a net there to catch them." After Vietnam, Malek was sent to Hawaii for the last year of his military career. He transferred to the Finance Corps ("I decided there was no sense running around on infantry maneuvers for another year") and took a civilian job selling encyclopedias from door to door at night. He became the best encyclopedia salesman on the island, earning $300 a week (in 1961). He also worked part time selling used cars and enrolled in a business-school correspondence course. He took Sunday afternoons off.

ARE YOU IN THE RIGHT PLACE?

When Fred Malek got out of the Army, he went to Harvard to get an MBA and then went to work for McKinsey and Company, a leading firm of management consultants. He thus put himself in the kind of situation from which successful careers develop. What are *you* doing right now? Is it plausible to expect that it will lead to the kind of career you want?

Before you can answer the latter question, you must

have established your own career goals, and to establish *those* intelligently, you must consider what kind of person you are. What can you do well? What will make you happy?

Being able to answer those questions thoughtfully is a basic prerequisite of success. People who succeed know what they can do and what they cannot. They know, in sum, who they are.

Those who do not succeed haven't a clue. Whenever I interview people, I ask them to describe themselves. You ought to hear some of them flounder. They say things like "Well, I am five foot eleven with brown hair and blue eyes." What a silly comment! Those who cannot explain their own strengths—generally because they haven't given the subject sufficient thought—will never be successful. Only when they understand what they can do can they play to those strengths. Only when they understand what they can't do can they go to work on correcting, or compensating for, their weaknesses.

Philip Smith, the talented president and CEO of General Foods and vice chairman of Philip Morris, is not good with details. "I knew this about myself a long time ago," he says. "On math tests, I'd get the concept right away, but I had to do all the problems three or four times, until I finally got convergence. In business school I took a lot of finance and accounting, and it was nearly the death of me.

"The whole early part of my career was spent fighting to make sure I didn't screw up on details, and doing things over and over to make sure I did them right." As a young brand manager responsible for detailed budget allocations, Smith traded one of his assistant brand managers for a statistical clerk—an unusual move that gave him the support he needed.

Smith's executive strengths far outweighed his weaknesses, and he relied on those as he rose to the top of General Foods. One position he held on the path to the presidency was that of chief financial officer. When he told his family about that job, his son objected, "Dad, you can't do that. You can't even add."

"There are a lot of people in the office who can add," Smith replied. *"I'm* not going to worry about the adding."

PICKING A JOB

Many jobs, particularly first jobs, are accepted simply because they are offered. This can be a terrible mistake. Jobs should be *selected,* not accepted. And one should begin by selecting a career one enjoys. (You may not enjoy every job on your career path, but every job—even the distasteful ones—should show promise of leading to jobs you do like.) If you are offered a great opportunity in the marketing department of General Motors, but you really want to work in the motion-picture industry or on Wall Street, pass it up. Your career is not "just a job"; it's your life. Nothing will make you more miserable—or more prone to fail—than a career you hate. It's hard enough to succeed in business if you *like* your work; it's almost impossible if you don't.

PICKING AN INDUSTRY

By the time you are thirty, at the latest, you should have decided what industry you want to be in—and be in it. Choosing an industry is likely to be a lifetime commitment. Once a career is launched in a particular field, the chances of transferring your skills to a totally different industry are slim (though not nonexistent). Experience and specific knowledge do matter. When we at Korn/Ferry get an assignment to find an executive for an aerospace company, say, we rarely if ever even consider individuals who are not already in the aerospace field. Rarely does a company want to gamble on a manager from an unrelated field, no matter how smart he is.

There are, of course, exceptions to this. Emerging industries like health care have had to fish in foreign waters in their search for management professionals. Highly entrepreneurial technology companies have sought talent from companies recognized for their marketing savvy. A lot of so-called "inter-industry" moves, however, are based upon a misperception of what industries people are actually in. A switch from cosmetics to dog food, for example, may not really be an industry switch at all. Both cosmetics and dog foods are packaged goods, and the merchandising techniques for them are very similar. When you are picking your industry, take a broad view of it, and figure out what industry you really are in.

Compensation levels should not generally be the most important factor in selecting an industry in which to work, but it is still of interest to see how the salaries of top executives compare in various fields. There is a significant difference, as our survey showed.

Table 2–1

**AVERAGE ANNUAL COMPENSATION OF
SENIOR EXECUTIVES BY INDUSTRY**
(1987 DOLLARS)

Retail	$265,000
Industrial	$247,000
Transportation	$229,000
Diversified Financial	$226,000
Insurance	$206,000
Commercial Banking	$177,000

In picking a field, do not reject out of hand the much-maligned "rust bowl" industries in favor of new high-tech ventures, which often produce more hype than profit. America's basic manufacturing sector—steel and other metals, chemicals, paper, defense—are essential to the health of our high-tech and service industries and essential to our nation's security as well. They will not be allowed to die, and they needn't even stay sick. We have already seen effective management (look at Iacocca) revivify selected "dying" companies. I am convinced that there will be tremendous opportunities in the 1990s for young managers who can help scrape the rust off the rust bowl.

Another industry worthy of consideration is the "nonindustry" of management consulting. Many of the brightest graduates of the top business schools opt for this profession, and for good reason. Consulting can shoot you into the top levels of business on a fast track. "If you go into consulting, you go in at a level at which you are interfacing with senior management on interesting problems on a regular basis," says Gary Wilson, who went to work for a small consulting firm after getting his MBA from Wharton. "It gives you a senior-management mindset. You mingle with the great, and you might be selected by the great to do something. It's a shortcut to the top." I know that's true, because it was for me.

Whatever industry you pick, be in the one you want to be in as early in your career as possible. I have seen too many people go unhappily through life because they are not working where they want to work. In such circumstances, they cannot possibly succeed.

PICKING A SPECIALTY

In a 1979 Korn/Ferry survey of senior executives, a plurality said that finance and accounting was the fastest route to the top in the corporate world. These responses came at the tail end of an era in which the number-cruncher had been king.

In our current survey, finance/accounting has fallen off its pedestal (although it still ranks number two). Leading

Table 2–2

FUNCTIONAL AREA
NAMED AS FASTEST ROUTE TO THE TOP

	TODAY	TEN YEARS FROM NOW
Marketing/Sales	34%	27%
Finance/Accounting	25%	21%
General Management	24%	23%
Professional/Technical	7%	13%
Production/Manufacturing	5%	5%
International	1%	4%
Personnel	1%	1%

the way as the fastest route to the top is now marketing and sales.

This is entirely appropriate. The mystique of the number-cruncher has diminished as executives have come to realize that if you don't have a good product to sell and an effective program for marketing it on a world-wide scale, you won't *have* any numbers to crunch. On today's intensely competitive international scene, marketing quality products is the paramount requirement for corporate success.

You should take this into consideration when deciding which functional area of management to enter. Not surprisingly, the largest number of our surveyed executives (44 percent) identify their current function as "general management." But only 4 percent began their careers in general management. The rest moved over from marketing, or finance, or another specialized area as their careers matured and their responsibilities increased. This is the way a career develops. (It is worth noting, however, that only 25 percent of those senior executives who started out in marketing remain in marketing, while 64 percent of those who started in finance/accounting remain in that area. Thus senior executives who began their careers in finance were more likely than others to retain their original specialty *and to secure senior executive status in so doing.*)

Marketing now seems to have achieved the place it deserves on the career ladder, but some other functions remain unfortunately neglected. Production, manufacturing, and technical areas are not considered fast routes to the top, and a young person would probably be making a mistake by entering one of those fields. To most bright young people, this probably does not appear to be a problem. How many kids come out of the Harvard Business School aching to manage a factory?

This is, however, a problem for America. It has been said, with some justification, that too many of the executives who run large American companies today do not understand how their own products are made. The emphasis on marketing and finance, accompanied by the trend toward establishing overseas assembly plants, has put much of American industry in the position of buying its manufacturing services much as it buys its advertising or office decoration. Given the present worldwide emphasis on technological innovation, this is a potentially dangerous state of affairs.

There is some indication that the pendulum is now swinging the other way. Asked to predict what will be the fastest route to the top ten years from now, more executives named technical areas. For the moment, young people might be well advised to study engineering or some other technical field and perhaps even work in it—but not for too long—and then move into marketing or general management. They will be better off for the move, and their company will be better off for their backgrounds.

PICKING A COMPANY

In 1954, Ray Hay, now chairman of the LTV Corporation, came out of the Navy and decided to look for a sales job in the up-and-coming data-processing-equipment industry. A thorough man, he interviewed with IBM, National Cash Register, Burroughs, Addressograph-Multigraph, and other companies. Each one offered him a job. "The question then became: Which one do I go to work for?" Hay recalls. He sat down with a friend and considered his options. "We reviewed the companies, and what we knew about them, and what their products were, and so on. We narrowed it down to three—Burroughs, NCR, and IBM. But we concluded that IBM was not a company for me, because the kind of business and structure they had was not in keeping with my personality, which is a little bit more aggressive. And selling there would probably not be as satisfying to me, because IBM involved longer-term big-item sales rather than frequent smaller sales. I thought I would probably enjoy a business where I could do something and see the results and then move on to another sale and get more successes instead of making one big deal once or twice a year.

"So that brought it down to Burroughs and NCR. And I picked NCR, because I thought it had better products and a better reputation.

"It also offered five dollars more a week. And I didn't have to change trains."

Never underestimate the subway factor in a New Yorker's job choice. But, that aside, Hay's deliberations are a model of how one ought to decide what company to work for. He took into account each company's product line, solvency, and potential as well as the mesh between his personality and the company's. Other factors worth considering were described in a *Fortune* article on job-hunting by recent business-school graduates: "Armed with business-research publications such as Moody's and Standard & Poor's, the shrewdest among them studied prospective employers' profit records and growth potential, and checked into such things as corporations' reputations for internal promotions and the average age of upper management."

Going to work for a company that is on the brink of bankruptcy, or in the process of merging, or vulnerable to a takeover has obvious risks. But some other important factors are not so obvious:

The Name-Brand Factor
Looking down the road toward future career moves, it often pays to have worked at companies that other people have heard of. If *you* were hiring a veteran sales manager, would you be more interested in someone who had worked at General Mills or someone from the Killer Bee Honey Corporation?

The Size Factor
Here is the drawback of large, established companies: big companies are, above all, big. It is possible to get a good job at one and then disappear. "I sure wouldn't like to be thrown into the bottom of the pit and have to fight my

way out of it," says Albert Snider, executive vice president, operations, of Avnet, Inc., who once quit Honeywell for a job with a smaller company. Honeywell had
offered him a promotion and had him on a list of "high-
potentials." "I guess I might have moved up," Snider acknowledges, "but, my God, they've got three hundred
thousand people to choose from." It's quite likely Snider
would have reached the top ranks at Honeywell, but, in a
smaller company, he achieved a position of major responsibility much more quickly.

Employees in newer, smaller companies almost automatically have more visibility and responsibility than
their peers in larger firms. Executives must of necessity
take on a number of different functions and have a broad
view of the entire corporation. The learning potential is
boundless.

And so is the growth potential. Much of the excitement
and revitalization of American business today is taking
place in mid-sized companies, and not just in the high-
tech field. You don't have to be a software engineer or a
computer wizard to find a spot in a coming firm. High-
growth companies are springing up in virtually every industry, even such unglamorous ones as tires and
industrial solvents. You can grow with them.

Often, joining a small organization is a good way of
putting oneself in the way of fate. When Marshall Manley
(now president of The Home Group and former chairman
of the management committee of the law firm of Finley,
Kumble, Wagner, Heine, Underberg, Manley & Casey) finished law school in 1965, he sorted through several good
job offers and elected to go to work for a small law firm in
California. "In California," he explains, "small firms did
big cases, whereas in New York only big firms did big
cases. I thought this would be an opportunity to get in on
the ground floor. I thought I could position myself in the
right niche to grow with the firm and would have more of
an opportunity to get to the forefront faster."

And that's what happened. In 1965, a major bank in San
Francisco failed, and Manley's firm represented depositors

with accounts larger than the federally insured limit. It turned out to be an important and immensely complex case, and Manley, at age twenty-five, was picked to handle it. "It was somewhat different from what most new lawyers do when they first come into firms," points out Manley. "I was picked because I was one of the few people there. There were only eight lawyers in the firm, and I was a litigator. It was a break for me. I got involved in something very important, and I had a chance to show whether I was good or bad."

Manley was good. He pursued reimbursement for his clients under a novel legal theory and won a settlement of $60 million. "I got a reputation for handling the big case," he says. "I began to understand how to handle a big case. And I got a reputation for success."

There is also a heightened risk, however, to working in a small firm or corporation. Because you are so visible, if you are not good (or get a bad break), you will bomb out a lot faster than if you worked for a larger company.

The Corporate-Culture Factor
"Corporate culture" has become a bit of a buzzword lately. One chief executive officer, *Business Week* reported, turned to his president after attending a seminar on the topic and enthused, "This corporate culture stuff is great. I want a culture by Monday."

That's not exactly the way it works. Although corporate cultures (and every organization has one) do reflect the tastes of chief executive officers, they evolve over time. They are the sum total of many aspects of the corporate environment: the way people dress, the way they act (on and off the job), the kind of management style that is encouraged, the number of work hours that is expected. Some of these items are trivial; others are significant. All will affect whether or not you are happy at a particular company.

Some aspects of corporate culture are obvious and incontrovertible. If everybody in the top ranks of a company went to Yale and you did not, you might want to consider working elsewhere. Ditto if everyone is over six feet tall and you are not (yes, some companies like to hire and promote tall people). But don't worry if everybody is a Republican and you are not. Most top executives do tend to be Republicans, but there are many notable exceptions, and big companies actually need executives who are active in both major parties. Politics and business come together at certain levels, and it is in a company's interest to employ people who are on good terms with both sides. So it's okay to be a Democrat, even if you get a little lonely during political discussions at the office.

Far less significant attributes than political convictions can be far more damaging or helpful. The most easily noticed aspect of corporate culture is probably the dress code, like IBM's famous "white shirts only" rule. IBM officially denies that it has, or has ever had, such a policy, but there sure are a lot of people wearing white shirts over there. IBM chairman Thomas Watson, Sr., told the writer Peter Drucker in 1939 that he insisted his salesmen wear dark suits and white shirts in an attempt to bolster their self-respect and raise their standard in the community, where salesmen were generally held in low regard. "I want my IBM salesmen to be people to whom their wives and their children can look up," he said. "I don't want their mothers to feel that they have . . . to dissimulate when they are being asked what their son is doing." Mothers are proud to have their sons selling for IBM nowadays, but the white-shirt wearing persists. One IBM salesman recently told *The New York Times* that when he wore a blue shirt to work one day, his boss asked him, "Jeff, are you selling to the Air Force this morning?"

At Avon, chairman Hicks Waldron requires employees to use Avon products as much as possible, including those of the company's James River Traders clothing subsidiary. "One problem with this edict," N. R. "Sonny" Kleinfeld of *The New York Times* reported, "is that James River Traders is not known for the exceptional breadth of its tie collection, and Avon executives sometimes show up at a meeting sporting identical neckwear."

Dress codes and the like are sometimes not as trivial as

they seem. "At General Motors, good appearance meant conservative dress," said John DeLorean, who once was a top G.M. executive, in the book *On a Clear Day You Can See General Motors.* "In my very first meeting as a G.M. employee in 1956 at Pontiac, half the session was taken up in discussion about some vice-president downtown at headquarters who was sent home that morning for wearing a brown suit. Only blue or black suits were tolerated then. I remember thinking that was silly. But in those days I followed the rules. . . .

"The corporate rule was dark suits, light shirts and muted ties. I followed the rule to the letter, only I wore stylish Italian-cut suits, wide-collared off-white shirts and wide ties.

" 'Goddamnit, John,' [my boss would] yell. 'Can't you dress like a businessman? And get your hair cut, too.'

"My hair was ear length with sideburns. I felt both my clothes and my hair style were contemporary but not radical, so I told him:

" 'General Motors' business—selling annual styling changes—makes this a fashion business. And what the hell do you know about fashion? Most of these guys around here wear narrow-lapeled suits and baggy pants with cuffs that are four inches above their shoes.' "

(Ultimately, DeLorean had troubles at G.M, and elsewhere, that had little to do with the way he looked.)

In most cases, surely, wearing a white shirt, or a dark suit, or even a tie with a duck on it, is no great hardship if that's what a company demands. Usually, the company will not formally *demand* anything. But look around; check out the chairman's picture in the annual report; you'll get the idea.

You may have to look a little harder to uncover more fundamental aspects of corporate culture. Sometimes when we are interviewing a candidate for a job, we will ask, "What kind of management style do you personally respond to?"

"Well," he'll reply, "I like to be told what my goals are and then left alone."

We say, "How would you feel about a boss who tends to

check in with you twice a day to see how you're doing?"

He says, "You mean, really?"

"Really," we say.

And he says, "Well, I don't think I could live very well with that."

But there are companies that operate like that, and if *you* couldn't live with it, working at such a place would make you very unhappy, a lot more unhappy than having to wear your blue suit.

Some companies are democratic, and others are autocratic. Some companies are relaxed and organized, and others thrive on a crisis atmosphere: employees are supposed to look as if they were in a constant work frenzy. In some companies, everybody takes off his jacket and loosens his tie as soon as he walks in the door. In others, people stay suited up all day. In some companies it is a badge of honor to work late into the night; in others they think you're incompetent if you can't get your work done by 5:30. *Fortune* once profiled a chief executive who was renowned for calling his employees at all hours of the day and night, for phoning them at home and dragging them off golf courses. "If they consider it a sacrifice," he said, "then they are at the wrong company." Indeed.

Companies differ as well in their attitudes toward employees' private lives. "The fact that I had been divorced, was a health nut and dated generally younger actresses and models didn't set well with the corporate executives or their wives," said John DeLorean. "I was being resented because my style of living violated an unwritten but widely revered precept that said no personality could outshine General Motors. The executives were supposed to be just as gray and almost as lifeless as the corporate image."

Larry Horner, the chairman of KPMG Peat Marwick, suffered a temporary setback to his career in 1972 when he got divorced. "It wasn't very fashionable in those days," he says. "There was a fair amount of questioning among the senior partners about the divorce situation, as to whether I could continue to be as effective....I had to, in a sense, re-prove myself." Horner did so, and ended up chairman, but he still recalls thinking that his treatment "was very unfair."

This kind of corporate attitude has liberalized in recent years. Where once some companies refused to hire divorced people, or even single people, today you can generally take your "best friend" to a company social event, and no one will raise an eyebrow.

The mosaic of company attitudes—on sex, suits, work hours, management style, and all the rest—adds up to its corporate culture, and its corporate culture is a fact of life. "The obvious dilemma," Walter Kiechel III wrote in *Fortune*, is "how much is merely taking on the patina of top management and how much is surrendering your individuality? If your new peers are, for example, a bunch of Ivy League milksops, do you think twice about mentioning your bowling scores? If they're all burr-headed ex–Marine commandos, do you go easy on the big words and the Nuit de Wimp cologne?"

The answer is, must be, yes. The company will not adapt to suit you. You are going to have to adapt to suit it. (This may be harder than you think; you cannot change what you are.) Corporate culture is set by the people at the top. Once you become chairman of the board, you can alter it any way you like. Until then, if you are not comfortable with a company's culture, stay away. The only alternative is to become the local iconoclast, and that's a very risky way to go.

THE LUCK FACTOR

Let us consider Cyrus and the others who acquired and founded kingdoms.... They do not seem to have had from fortune anything other than opportunity. Fortune, as it were, provided the matter but they gave it its form; without opportunity their prowess would have been extinguished, and without such prowess the opportunity would have come in vain. Thus for the Israelites to be ready to follow Moses...it was necessary for him to find them, in Egypt, enslaved and oppressed....For Romulus to become king of Rome and founder of his country, he had to have left Alba and been exposed to die when he was born.

Niccolò Machiavelli, *The Prince*

And for Darryl Hartley-Leonard to become president of Hyatt Hotels, it was necessary that he walk into a motel in City of Commerce, California, one summer day in 1964.

Hartley-Leonard, then nineteen years old, had recently arrived in the United States from his native England, where he had graduated from a hotel school in Blackpool. In the U.S., he sent handwritten letters seeking a job to Sheraton, to Hilton, and to other hotel companies.

"And I got the standard rejection letters," he recalls. "They all said, 'I am sorry but we have nothing for a person with your qualifications.' So I was disillusioned, and I was totally out of money. And I wandered into the Hyatt House Motor Hotel, which was just opening up in City of Commerce, a little town outside Los Angeles on the Santa Ana Freeway. It had one hundred and fifty-six rooms. And in the lobby of the hotel—and this is probably the single key thing that affected me—I met a guy called Pat Foley. He was thirty-two years old, and a little crazy, and in his first job as a general manager. His office was behind the front desk. And he happened to walk out. He asked me what I was doing there. And he gave me a job as relief desk clerk."

Once in every successful executive's lifetime, he or she must be at the right place at the right time. That moment in 1964 was Hartley-Leonard's right time; that modest hotel was his right place. He didn't know it yet, but his life had just been changed.

Hartley-Leonard and Foley worked together and got along well, and as the two men moved elsewhere in the Hyatt organization, they stayed in touch. Foley rocketed toward the top. As he did, says Hartley-Leonard, he "was instrumental in watching over my career." When Foley became executive vice president, he played a role in assigning Hartley-Leonard to manage the company's flagship hotel in Atlanta. When Foley became president, he was involved in promoting Hartley-Leonard to executive vice president. Hartley-Leonard became president himself in 1986, at the age of forty; Foley is now chairman.

Would Hartley-Leonard be Hyatt's president today if Foley had been home sick that day in 1964?

"It would depend," acknowledges Hartley-Leonard. "I was so impressionable that had I had the wrong mentor with the wrong style of management, probably not."

EVERYBODY IS "LUCKY"

Every successful person I know says he or she has been very lucky. Luck is, in fact, named third (after hard work and ambition) as the single most important factor in successful careers. But all this talk of luck is somewhat misleading. In the case of almost every successful person, luck was a *necessary* but not a *sufficient* condition for his or her success. As Machiavelli said, without those individuals' own prowess, their opportunities would have come in vain. All those who have succeeded say they were, at least once, in the right place at the right time. But almost without fail, if you examine the circumstances carefully, you will see that they made very sure they were in the right place.

Sometimes individuals' roles in creating their own luck is not immediately obvious, especially when their good fortune is of the sort we might call "general luck." A person enters the work force when the economy is booming, or goes to work for a particular company when *it* is booming, or benefits in an unforeseeable way from some other external economic or political factor.

Thomas Watson, Sr., of IBM almost went bankrupt

twice during the Depression, reports Peter Drucker. "What saved him and spurred IBM sales... were two New Deal laws: the Social Security Act in 1935 and the Wage-Hours Act of 1937–38. They mandated records of wages paid, hours worked, and overtime earned by employees, in a form in which the employer could not tamper with the records. Overnight they created markets for the tabulating machines and time clocks that Thomas Watson Sr. had been trying for long years to sell with only moderate success."

The young Lee Iacocca also benefited from a boom not of his making. His first job at Ford, in 1947, was in sales. "My timing was lucky," he writes. "There had been no car production during the war, so between 1945 and 1950, demand was high. Every new car was sold at list price—if not more.... Although I had a lowly position, the backlog for new cars gave my job a lot of clout."

Ray Hay, who went to work for National Cash Register in 1954, found himself selling automatic accounting machines at a time when "there was a lot of opportunity, because there were a lot of old key-driven machines and a lot of hand systems" which were long overdue for modernization.

Like many young women in recent years, Mary Cunningham (of Bendix fame) benefited from a social and political movement. Her memoir opens with the words: "I was a woman who was in the right place at the right time. During the spring of my second year at Harvard Business School, I had thirty-two job offers from investment-banking firms, management-consulting firms and Fortune 500 companies. It was a time when corporations were hungry for bright-eyed, ambitious young MBAs and especially eager for women."

PERSONAL LUCK

The second variety of luck is personal and specific. It has nothing to do with general economic conditions. Like the luck of Hartley-Leonard, it has to do with who walks through a particular door at a particular moment, who gets a stomachache and is late for which meeting. According to *Fortune,* the career of the well-known financier Felix Rohatyn got a crucial boost because he had a date one night in the summer of 1949. Then a physics major at Middlebury College, Rohatyn had a summer job at Lazard Frères, the investment-banking house, in New York. He decided to stick around the office after normal hours that night "because I had a date in midtown and it wouldn't have made sense to go home and then come back." André Meyer, the legendary Lazard partner, wandered by. "André saw me there, a young man dedicated to his work. He thought I must really have something and asked if I wanted to work at Lazard." Several years later, Rohatyn was a partner in the firm.

Larry Horner, now chairman of KPMG Peat Marwick, went to work in that accounting firm's Kansas City office right after college. During his first year there, he was assigned to join an auditing team handling a client in Wichita. After a few days, the senior accountant in charge of the team decided he wanted to go home. "The firm looked around," says Horner, "and they really didn't have a better solution, so they let me take charge of the audit, which was a job much above where I would have been logically and probably above my competency. But I made it through, with a lot of supervision and help. And therefore skipped a number of levels and moved ahead rather rapidly from there on....It was just a pure stroke of luck that I happened to be sitting there."

BUT IS IT LUCK?

But is this really luck we're talking about? Did that long-ago date ensure Rohatyn's success? Did the homesickness of his superior in Wichita guarantee that Larry Horner would rise to the top of Peat Marwick?

Of course not.

Perhaps, occasionally, luck is all. A man overhears a (legal) stock tip, he buys the stock, he makes a fortune. But one lucky break cannot make a career.

"You can have luck," says Larry Horner. "You go to Las

Vegas and hit a big jackpot, and the smartest thing you did was put the money in and pull the handle. That's not the kind of luck I'm talking about. It's having an opportunity—or luck, if you will—and then being able to take advantage of it.... Maybe it's my ego, but I like to think I had the ability to take advantage of [what happened in Wichita] and convert that opportunity."

That is exactly what happened. Horner used his lucky break the way a judo expert uses the weight of an opponent. The opponent approaches and lunges; the judo expert seizes him and uses his own weight and force to send him flying where the judo expert wants him to go.

Let's take a second look at some of the examples of "luck" recounted above:

Ray Hay did enter the automated-accounting-machine business at a time when it was taking off, but he didn't decide to enter that business by picking it out of a hat. He saw that it was ready to take off; that's *why* he went into it.

Larry Horner, *after* his lucky break in Wichita, worked harder than anyone else in the Kansas City office of Peat Marwick. An accountant has a theoretical limit of 2,080 billable hours in a year (40 times 52); in some years, working overtime, Horner billed more than 2,300 hours. He was driven, as every successful person must be, by ambition. "There was no question in my mind, from the day I joined the firm, that I wanted to run it," he says.

Darryl Hartley-Leonard may have gotten his big break —the assignment to manage Hyatt's flagship hotel in Atlanta—partly because of his old association with Pat Foley; but if he had not done a great job there, he might be back in City of Commerce today instead of sitting atop the Hyatt corporate structure in Chicago.

Those who succeed are not passive about their luck. When it arrives, they, first of all, recognize it, and then they do something about it. Lee Iacocca compounded his luck—having become a Ford salesman when demand was high—by working hard at becoming an extraordinary salesman. Thomas Watson, Sr., was able to capitalize on the newly created need for business machines because he had been working in the field for decades; he was the business equivalent of the actor who labors unheralded in Off-Off-Broadway shows for twenty years and then becomes an "overnight" success.

Those who succeed upon getting their "lucky" breaks have also, it often turns out, deliberately put themselves in spots where lightning is likely to strike. In my own career, I worked early on as a management consultant at Peat Marwick. In that position, I urged the firm to offer new consulting services and then went to work in the profit centers that were created to provide them. Being one of the few people in a new area left me far more exposed to "luck" than remaining with hundreds of people in an established division would have.

One of the big breaks in the career of Gary Wilson, now executive vice president of Disney, came shortly after he graduated business school and went to work for a small consulting firm called Checchi & Company. Checchi was an investor in a major Philippine holding company and had a contract to supply the Philippine company's chief financial officer. "This job, to go to the Philippines, was considered the best job in the whole [Checchi] company," Wilson says. The man who was doing it suddenly got sick; a replacement was required immediately. Wilson got the job—"a job I had absolutely no business doing," he says—and it launched his career. At the age of twenty-five, he was suddenly "a big wheel in a big company in a country where I was mingling with all the big wheels in the country." Wilson became involved in organizing a general refinancing of the company, in selling sugar mills, buying a construction company, and establishing a major sugar-trading operation. "I learned more during that five years than I ever learned before or will ever learn again in that short a period of time," he says. He eventually returned to Checchi & Company as its number-two man.

"I was very lucky that the guy got sick," Wilson says. But Wilson had clearly given luck a nudge. As a graduating business student, he had deliberately chosen Checchi

& Company over other potential employers because it was small and entrepreneurial. He liked the fact that it combined consulting with managing its own investments. He also noticed that no one in the firm except him had any training in finance. "I had positioned myself," he says. "I think one lesson you learn in life is you make your own luck. If you position yourself where the probabilities are in your favor, like in a poker game, you're going to win."

Frequently the "luck" of successful executives is so obviously self-generated that it can't be called luck at all. Listen to Jane Evans describing a milestone on her road to the presidency of the I. Miller fashion chain:

"I was at one point the buyer of handbags and accessories, and I was literally at the right place at the right time. There was a fashion change taking place; women were moving from large handbags to much smaller Italian handbags. I made a trip to Europe and was very fortunate that I spoke Italian and was able to deal directly with a lot of manufacturers that no one else was able to deal with. Also, I was willing to get on a train and go out to Rimini and out to the wilds of Italy [to see manufacturers] who weren't represented by agents. I had to track them down. I'd see a style and get their address, call them up and make an appointment, and go out and see them. By dealing directly with a lot of these firms, I was able to get unique product and develop a very good handbag business for I. Miller, ahead of the rest of the competition in New York."

Evans claims she was just "in the right place at the right time." But was it sheer luck that she had learned Italian and that she had the determination and imagination to chase down obscure handbag manufacturers all over the Italian countryside? Hardly.

Another way to consider the relationship between successful careers and luck is to look at what happened when successful executives encountered *bad* luck.

In the late 1940s, Harry Gray was making between $13,000 and $15,000 a year as a bus salesman—a hell of a lot of money in those days. "That went fine," Gray says, "until the Korean War broke out, and all of a sudden the steel allocated to buses was cut in half. All of a sudden what I made was cut in half because I wasn't going to get the product."

Gray didn't get depressed. He got out. He quit his job and went to work at Greyhound, which had been one of his customers. If it hadn't been for the Korean War, Gray says, "I could have ended up running a bus-manufacturing company." Instead (after a successful stint at Greyhound and many good years at Litton Industries) he ended up running United Technologies. Gray did not succumb to his bad luck. He left it behind him and went looking for good luck. He was smart about his pursuit of it, and tenacious, and ambitious. Like every single one of the smart, hardworking, ambitious, successful people I know, Gray eventually got "lucky."

PREPARING FOR LUCK

If you are going to succeed, you must be in the right place at the right time at least once in your life. But you must also have prepared yourself to grab that opportunity when it comes, to have the wit to respond when luck beckons. Millions of people have had luck stare them in the face and failed to take advantage of it. Those who succeed seize the moment.

"I am a great believer that if you work hard as hell, you do get lucky," says Ray Dempsey, chairman of the European American Bank, whose own career involves a single lucky moment while waiting for an elevator—a "lucky" moment made possible by his lifelong habit of hard work.

"There is one single event in my life," he says, "that I took advantage of which had more to do with my success than anything. I was a young credit analyst with Bankers Trust, and a guy named Al Brittain ran the energy group there. I got a call that said, 'Mr. Brittain is going to call on Standard Oil of California, and he is leaving tomorrow.

Would you write a memo about our relationship with Standard Oil?' I said okay. The call came late in the afternoon, and I worked until ten or eleven o'clock that night, put together an eight-page memorandum, had it all typed, gave it to my boss, who gave it to Brittain, and that was it. That was a Wednesday. On Monday I happened to be standing at the elevator bank. And Al Brittain came by. I really didn't know him. I knew who he was. He was a senior vice president. That was very close to being God. But he came by and he said, 'Ray, I just want to tell you that that memo you did was really tremendous. It gave me everything I needed. And I really appreciate that you would work that hard to get it done on such short notice.'

"I have always felt I was lucky standing there at the elevator at the same time he was.... I was recognized by him as being aggressive and doing a good job. And then I was given opportunities, because of that recognition, to do some challenging things."

In the years that followed the elevator meeting, Brittain and Dempsey became close associates, professionally and personally. Brittain rose to become chairman of Bankers Trust, and Dempsey became executive vice president before he moved to another bank. While he still looks back at that elevator meeting as "lucky," Dempsey recognizes as well what lay behind that moment. "I have always felt that if I had just slapped together a one-page memo, I wouldn't have made an impression.... All my life, I've been a very hard worker. I just think that if you are supposed to take five steps, you should really take seven or eight, *always*. Just keep going farther. I did it in this case." And it led to his "luck."

This is a very familiar story in the careers of the successful. Luck does play a factor in people's lives, propelling a few to the top and leaving many behind. But as the great scientist Louis Pasteur said, "Chance favors the prepared mind."

The life of any individual who makes it to the top is one of constant preparation. All that follows in the rest of this book, all the career advice, all the tips on changing jobs and getting promoted, can be seen simply as lessons in how to prepare yourself for the day you meet *your* Mr. Brittain at the elevator, and how to put yourself in luck's way in case it is a little slow in coming.

PART 3

RECONNOITERING THE CORPORATION

WHENEVER I make a speech or other public appearance, people come up to me afterward and hand me their résumés. They are hoping, I presume, that their career histories will be coded into the Korn/Ferry computer and that someday—presto!—their phones will ring with fabulous job offers. Once in a rare while, this actually happens, but in general the practice of casting one's résumé upon the waters is indicative of an overly passive attitude toward improving one's career. You should not be sitting around waiting for a marvelous job to come to you; *you* should be moving toward *it*.

The people we do place in senior executive positions have all taken active roles in promoting themselves. From their very first days in any new job, they have been thinking about a) their next promotions, and b) their overall careers.

You should not begin *any* job at any point in your career without knowing:

- Why you have taken it.
- What it can lead you to within the next two years.
- How it fits into your total career plan.

To gain this knowledge, a new employee must make a deliberate effort to learn about the corporation in which he or she works, and the role assigned to his or her job by the corporate structure. Undertaking this kind of corporate reconnaissance, like an agent landed in unfamiliar territory, is a prerequisite to moving up the ladder within the company.

MOVE UP, NOT OUT

You will notice that I said *within* the company. The younger generation today (and the not-so-young one as well) seems enthralled by the idea of switching jobs. The prospect of hopping to other companies beckons to them with promises of shortcuts to promotions and raises.

I certainly do not want to be in the position of opposing all job changes. Facilitating such changes is how I make my living, and I spend a great deal of time persuading reluctant executives to move. There are indeed times when a job change is the best possible move for a rising executive (I will explain when and why in a later section). But most of the time, for most people, the glittering promises of job-hopping are illusory.

I have seen all too many people change jobs for 15-percent raises. If they had just stayed where they were, they would have had 10-percent raises within a few months, and another round of 10-percent raises a year after that. At their new jobs, they were not even considered for raises for a year and a half. By taking "higher-paying" jobs, they actually lost money.

Worse, I have seen people switch jobs without seriously considering how their new positions fit into their lifetime career plans. For a few extra dollars and the thrill of a jump, they have launched themselves onto time-wasting detours, leading away from where they really want to go.

Most successful careers in American corporations are built by staying put, not moving. Eighty percent of all job promotions are made from within. Earning big money is often a function of longevity.

These facts are evident in the careers of the senior executives in our survey. They have worked for their current employers for an average of seventeen years. Twenty-four percent of them have had no other employer. Their average number of employers has been only two.

Those who have changed jobs more than average actually earn *less* than those who have stayed put. Senior executives in the insurance industry, for example, who have had three or more employers earn an average of $166,413. Those who have had only one or two employers earn an average of $226,629.

Table 3–1

CURRENT SALARIES BY COMPANY OPERATIONS FOR LOW- AND HIGH-TURNOVER GROUPS
(1987 DOLLARS)

	OVERALL	LOW	HIGH
Commercial Banking	177,362	187,215	165,319
Insurance	205,827	226,629	166,413
Diversified Financial	225,534	233,198	218,965
Industrial	247,430	251,810	243,051
Transportation	228,818	252,905	205,827
Retail	264,948	283,560	248,525

The survey also explains, however, why young executives may be lured by job-hopping. Early in their careers, those executives who changed jobs more often earned more than their stationary peers. At age twenty-five, high-turnover executives were earning 5 percent more than the low-turnover group. Within a few years, however, the tortoises passed the hares. The low-turnover group became the high-salary group.

There is, sadly, more to this story than money. Executives who move too many times may move themselves right out of employability. A thirty-five-year-old who thinks, "One more good job-hop and I've got it made," may be dangerously mistaken. One more job-hop and he may be dead. I constantly see people eliminated from consideration for desirable jobs because they have moved "too often"—which may mean three or four times in the past ten years.

Somewhat illogically, job changes *within* a company

Table 3–2

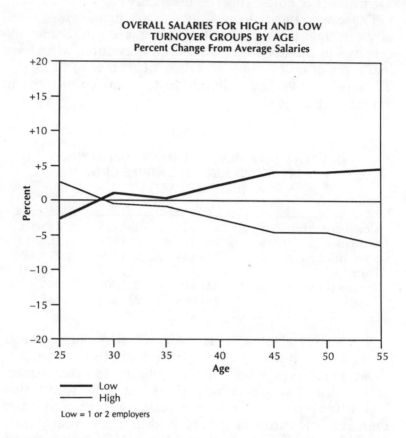

OVERALL SALARIES FOR HIGH AND LOW
TURNOVER GROUPS BY AGE
Percent Change From Average Salaries

Low = 1 or 2 employers

never count against you. If you had worked for ten companies in ten years, a potential employer would probably
consider you unhirable. If you'd had the same ten jobs
within a single company, the potential employer would
probably admire your "diverse background."

So think about moving up within your company, not
outside it. If you are competent and hardworking, some
promotions will inevitably come your way. But they will
come faster and better if you do some careful planning
and implement some simple strategies. Begin with some
basic intelligence-gathering.

FIND THE UPWARD PATH

When John Chamberlin, former president of Avon Products, completed an executive training program at General Electric in 1955, he elected to take a job there selling light bulbs. He had no particular interest in either selling or light bulbs—"It was certainly not what I wanted to do as a career," he says—but Chamberlin was smart enough to have done some important homework.

His ambition then (in retrospect, a modest one) was to become the marketing manager of one of General Electric's divisions. At the time, the traditional concept of marketing was changing. Marketing was coming to be seen as a combination of sales, advertising, service, market research, and production planning. But Chamberlin investigated the backgrounds of G.E.'s marketing managers and found that they all had one thing in common. "Whether they were in the housewares department, or the radio department, or the steam-turbine division," he recalls, "their background was in sales."

Chamberlin drew the obvious conclusion: "You didn't succeed in marketing in the General Electric Company unless you were in sales." So he sought, and got, his job selling light bulbs.

Chamberlin's reasoning was sound, and it remains sound today. There are certain historically proved paths to the top in any organization. This applies to relatively small organizational units, such as corporate divisions, as well as to companies' top command structures. Whether you are a management trainee or a vice president, you can and should discover which are the proved paths to the positions to which you aspire. It doesn't take much effort to find out what today's marketing managers, or senior vice presidents, were doing when they were at your level. Were they in sales? In finance? In planning? Do only marketing executives get promoted to top-management slots? Did all the division managers at one time work in production? The answers to these questions will vary from unit to unit and company to company. Once you have them, you can launch, or adjust, your career accordingly. I am constantly amazed at how many otherwise bright people fail to take these simple steps.

Like Chamberlin's co-workers, for example. Chamberlin himself had come out of Harvard Business School, and many of his fellow executive trainees had similarly impressive backgrounds. "A lot of them elected areas other than sales," Chamberlin says, "because they thought sales was beneath them. Sales was in low repute—*Death of a Salesman* was very popular about that time—and people with good intellectual capabilities would say, 'I'm going to go into other areas.' A lot of them didn't want to look at history, or, if they did, they said, 'I can break it. I can go around it.'" But not Chamberlin. He was just as unenthusiastic about selling as many of his peers. "But I said, 'Facts are facts. This is what's needed.'"

I faced a similar situation myself in my early days at the accounting firm of Peat Marwick. I was not a CPA. It was obvious that anyone who hoped to rise to a partnership in the firm had to be one. I had not taken the requisite accounting courses, but I didn't let that deter me from taking the CPA exam. I passed—and gaining my partnership became only a matter of time.

The same kind of facts were faced by Lee Iacocca at Ford in the late 1940s. Iacocca had studied engineering at Lehigh and Princeton and had been hired by Ford as an engineer. After nine months of engineering training there, he decided, "I wanted to stay at Ford, but not in engineering. I was eager to be where the real action was—marketing or sales." And he made the switch.

Chamberlin, like Iacocca, went on to enjoy a successful career, strengthened by his experience in an essential training ground. Both men looked for the upward path and put themselves on it. It is no harder to start out on that path than on any other. So why not start on the one that leads to the top of the mountain?

SEE THE BIG PICTURE

Your job is your job, and a prerequisite for any kind of success is to do it well. But do not get lost in your job. Never forget that it is a small part of a big canvas. Keep your eye on that larger canvas.

Donald Beall, the much-admired CEO of Rockwell International, learned this lesson from his father. "My dad, who probably graduated from ninth grade, was a small businessman and a self-taught student of business. He would say, 'If you put in extra effort to really understand the key issues and players, and learn more than just what is in front of your face—which ninety percent of the people will not do, no matter how well educated they are—that will be recognized.'"

Beall started his own career as a financial analyst in Ford's aerospace-electronics subsidiary, and he practiced what his father preached. "I made it my business to understand as best I could the entire business of that division, rather than just the little jobs I had. I spent a lot of time studying proposals that were going for new-business and technical reports, which was outside the scope of my job." Beall rose rapidly at Ford and became the youngest divisional controller the company had ever had, and he still kept looking at the bigger picture. "Because of my interest in the business, which was broader than just being controller, I operated very much as a deputy general manager."

This kind of outlook was formalized by Ray Hay, today the chairman of LTV, when he was a manager at Xerox (where he rose to the rank of executive vice president). "I created a 'wheel concept,'" he says. "I would explain to everybody that their job was twofold. They had two jobs. They were, say, chief financial officer, *and* they were assistant general manager. Or they were personnel manager, *and* they were assistant general manager."

Everybody was an assistant general manager.

"Everybody's job focused on the main job. If you did an excellent job as the controller but you did not do an excellent job of helping the service manager do his job better, to the degree that he required help or guidance from the controller's organization, or you did not use your function to achieve the objectives of the corporation, then I didn't care how good a job you did running your function; you were not doing the other job you had to do. You had to think beyond the point of just being a great controller. There are lots of great controllers. I am not interested in your being just a great controller. I want you to contribute to the management of the business."

Even young John Chamberlin, ensconced in his position as a light-bulb salesman, intuitively realized the importance of this attitude. "You've just got to get that sense in you of what an organization is, how big it is, what's happening. You just have to do that. You go into General Electric today, and there are some people who know nothing but the large-lamp department. That is their life. That is their world. The question is: What is *your* world?"

The answer is: If you want to get ahead, your world had better be as big as the company you work in.

And while you're at it, do not neglect the even bigger world outside. Economic, political, and social trends may, in the long run, affect your company's business more than any internal decisions. If you work in the oil industry, pay attention to what OPEC is up to. If your company owns a French subsidiary, it can't possibly hurt you to be aware of whether the socialists or conservatives are in ascendance in Paris and whether they are in the process of nationalizing or denationalizing major companies. (Both things happen in France, and they are not always done by the obvious party.) This kind of general reading will serve you better than reading only *Forbes* and *Fortune* and *Business Week*. The business press is repetitive; you don't have to read everything. Read *one* good business magazine and allot some of the time you save to more general reading; in news of the world at large you may find keys to the future of your business.

MESH YOUR GOALS

In investigating the world of your company, pay special attention to its goals. Every corporation has objectives, and every corporate unit has its own objectives. These may be sales goals, profit goals, production goals. You must determine what those objectives are, and make sure that your own work serves them.

Failing to do this can have disastrous consequences. You may be doing your job just great, doing it as well as it can possibly be done, and nobody cares, because it is not important to the goals of your unit. Incredibly, many people go about their jobs for years without ever asking, "What am I supposed to be doing?" They may be doing only half of what they ought to be, because they have never inquired directly what their boss wants of them, and he or she has failed to communicate in return.

"Sometimes I just want to stop some people around here and ask, 'Why are you doing what you're doing?'" says William Smithburg, CEO of Quaker Oats. "We are a *marketing*-driven company. Our primary decisions of a strategic and tactical nature are marketing-oriented, and every area of the Company has to understand that it plays a role in the marketing process. If we make the right decisions in that process—about market research, product development and marketing strategies—then we have a chance to succeed financially for the shareholders. If you make the wrong decisions in the marketing process, it doesn't matter what else you do. Even being the low-cost producer is not enough to save you. You could be the low-cost producer of Product X, but if you can't sell it, or it's improperly positioned, you're dead."

Now, if you are a bright young MBA at Quaker Oats, and you are concentrating, to the exclusion of all else, on trying to decrease the unit cost of crunchy granola bars by playing games in the grain-futures market, how far do you think you're going to go? Your goal might be appropriate for some other company; you are out of step at Quaker Oats.

Quaker Oats makes things easier for its employees; it lists its corporate objectives every year on page two of its annual report. (Number One is: "Be a leading marketer of strong consumer brands of goods and services.") Not all companies communicate so clearly, but it should not be too difficult anywhere to ascertain the goals of one's company and division. And you cannot operate intelligently until you do.

If you are working on a product line, you must know what the company is hoping to achieve with that product. Is it aiming for high market share? Or for a high profit-per-piece? If the product is losing ground, is the company committed to reviving it? Or is it interested only in an orderly retreat? If the latter, there's no point in knocking yourself out trying to line up new sales outlets. The answers to these questions may not be obvious from the point of view of a foot soldier in the marketing department. But even a foot soldier can find the answers with a little digging. Often they can be found simply by reading the company's own press releases, and articles about the company in *The Wall Street Journal* and other business periodicals. It is absolutely astounding how many people do not read the news about their own companies.

On a closer-to-home level, it should not be difficult to identify, via the office grapevine, the immediate goals of your own work unit. If your boss is under pressure to produce $5 million in profit this year, and it's going to be a tight squeeze, you had better know about it. (He might just *tell* you, but he might not.) If he is under such pressure, this would not be a great time to go see him with a brilliant new idea that would, in the short run, cost him $1 million. He may snap that he hates your idea and throw you out of his office, when the real problem is that he likes your idea too well; he simply cannot contemplate making any kind of new investment until the quarterly returns are in. If you're aware of what's going on, you can wait, or approach him in a different way, or even take your idea to somebody else (perhaps *his* boss). But you can't even begin to think about altering your strategy if you don't know about his objectives in the first place.

DISCOVER WHERE
THE ACTION IS

After two (successful) years as a light-bulb salesman for General Electric, John Chamberlin decided he wanted out. He had continued to study the affairs of G.E. the way a Sovietologist studies the Kremlin. "I've *always* been interested in the broad company, its organization and power structure," he says. "To me, that was always critical." Chamberlin had learned two things:

1. His probable future in light-bulb sales did not appeal to him. "I could see the way the division was structured. I could move up to be an assistant sales manager in a district, and then sales manager in a district. That was a good, solid, steady course, but I didn't want to do it."

2. There was a new, hotter opportunity available elsewhere in the company. "General Electric had started an internal management-consulting group that was made up of guys who had been marketing managers—high-level

guys—and a couple of 'runners,' younger guys who did the minor jobs. I thought, 'This is a growing opportunity.'" Chamberlin told a friend who worked in the department that he would like to join it.

Chamberlin's fellow light-bulb salesmen couldn't understand why he would walk away from a successful sales career. "They thought I was crazy," Chamberlin recalls. But he made the move anyway, and for good reason. The consulting group was a star within the G.E. organization. Chamberlin learned a lot there, and made valuable connections. His association with the group advanced his career in ways that staying in selling could not.

Sometimes the selection of a career path within a company is easy. Caroline Nahas, one of my partners at Korn/ Ferry, began her career as a college recruiter for Bank of America. She rose rapidly in the bank's personnel department, but she realized that the greatest personnel executive in the world would have a limited career at Bank of America. "In banking," she says, "personnel was not the main track. The mainstream of banking is lending and finance; so I made a transfer from personnel into finance, which was very unusual. I moved to the world banking division, where I was making loans to multinational corporations.

"It was a risk/benefit situation. The bank was taking a risk on me. I had performed extraordinarily well in personnel, but that's a totally different area. I was taking a risk in getting into a zone that did not have a high level of comfort for me. My first year in lending was extremely difficult. The kinds of terms that bankers throw around —'ratio analysis,' 'debt-to-equity'—those things meant nothing to me. I dived in and studied. It was like going back to school."

Nahas put in all the extra hours she had to and learned what she needed to learn. She was ambitious, so she had no choice. If she wanted to succeed in banking, she had to have experience in its core activity. She had recognized an elementary prerequisite for success.

Sometimes discovering the hot area within a company

requires more complex intelligence-gathering. Whatever it takes, it is worth the effort. A company reveals its future through the activities it chooses to encourage; being associated with those activities can give your career a major boost. To spot such hot areas, keep a lookout for the following signs:

- Which divisions are getting big budget increases?
- What activities and products are being promoted and discussed by senior executives?
- Are a disproportionate number of people being promoted to top jobs coming out of a single unit or area?
- What skills does the company seem to be seeking in the new people it is hiring? (Do you have those skills? Can you get them?)

Alertness to signs like these helped guide the career of Norman Blake, who is today chairman of Heller International Corporation and was rated by *Fortune* in 1986 as one of America's ten "most wanted managers." Blake, like Chamberlin, spent most of his career at General Electric, where he rose to the post of executive vice president of G.E. Credit before being recruited to run Heller. Early in his career at G.E., Blake spotted a hot trend within the corporation:

"When Reg Jones became chairman, one of the things that he was very interested in was developing strategic planning, and there was a tremendous push in terms of strategic planning within the corporation. The glamour approach to the business became strategic planning. I saw this in the corporate reorganizations and in the internal meetings and training programs that were being provided for senior management. They all made it clear that strategic planning was the wave of the future. I wanted to get on that boat.

"I didn't even know what strategic planning was," Blake admits. But it seemed interesting, and he thought it was something he could do, and it clearly was *the* thing to be doing at General Electric at that time.

With some difficulty, Blake wangled a lateral transfer to

a job as a sort of junior strategic planner in a division that repaired turbine generators, motors, and other industrial equipment. This was hardly G.E.'s most glamorous division—"It was one of their gruntier businesses," Blake says—but no matter, he had become a strategic planner.

The only remaining problem was that he still didn't know what that was. "I borrowed as many books as I could," he recalls. "They wouldn't sign me up for a planning class, so I gleaned information from wherever I could get it. A friend of mine had gone to one of the classes, and I asked him if he would send me his class books, and I'd Xerox them and send them back. So I kind of picked up this information."

Indeed he did. Blake figured out what a strategic planner was supposed to do, and he ended up doing it well. He put his grunty old division into profitable new businesses and eventually caught the eye of important people elsewhere in the company. Blake's career was launched—because he had spotted the action area within the company and made it his business to get there.

Every company has clearly favored paths to the top. Some paths have been favored historically, such as the traditional preference of the automobile companies and other heavy industries for executives with manufacturing and engineering experience. Some paths are favored because they are part of an emerging trend of the moment, as in the case of strategic planning at General Electric (which still emphasizes the discipline). An ambitious executive must be aware of what is happening within his or her company, what has happened in the past, and what is likely to happen in the future. These are not state secrets. A little digging can uncover them—and can make an enormous difference in the careers of those who make the effort to dig them out. It always pays to become associated with the activities a company values most highly.

PART 4

MOVING UP: LAYING THE GROUNDWORK

W̲E LIVE in an ambitious age. Everybody wants more—more money, more status, more job satisfaction— and everybody feels he or she is entitled to get it.

Things didn't use to be this way. Not so many years ago, people accepted the idea that society was tiered, that there were a high-income group and a lower-income group, with a substantial divide between them. Many people of intelligence and skill who worked in lower or middle management "knew" and accepted that they would never join the rarefied ranks of top executives.

Few people today are willing to accept the idea that they have to live modest lives. As higher education has become widely available and class barriers have lowered, Americans have articulated aggressively their desire for more of everything. All the people in the middle think they have a chance to reach the top, and it seems they are all trying to get there.

These new attitudes have been accompanied by corresponding changes in corporate promotion practices. In almost every industry, upward mobility is accepted and encouraged. Promotions come more quickly than they did in decades past. When Raymond Dempsey, now chairman of the European American Bank, began his career at Bankers Trust in 1957, he recalls, "In those days, if you got to be an assistant treasurer in ten years from the day you started, you were doing well." At that rate, no one had enough years in his life to become president. Dempsey himself spent "only" (!) five years as a credit investigator and credit analyst before being made an assistant treasurer; he spent four years in that job before becoming an assistant vice president. Today, such a pace seems tortoise-like. "It's like athletics," says Larry Horner, chief executive officer and chairman of the accounting firm of Peat Marwick. "They [corporate employees] run faster and jump higher than they did in my day."

And they compete like crazy. Moving up in American companies generally requires elbowing aside able competitors for every promotion. People are seeking jobs aggressively, and they are showing up well prepared.

To take an example from the top, when John Reed was chosen in 1984 to succeed Walter Wriston at the helm of Citicorp, he beat out at least two other major contenders for the job. After Reed's selection, Citicorp board member Irving Shapiro explained that Reed was picked because, "in a practical sense, he was batting .350 and the other two guys were batting .340." Certainly a very fine difference.

In any job you seek, those few percentage points, that fine difference, can make all the difference in the world. Any edge you can get might be the edge that gets you the job. A number of elementary edges—ones you should incorporate into your career from the beginning—are the subject of this section.

I have found in working with senior executives over the past twenty years that those who reach the top have been very calculating in their careers. They have, in a sense, adopted third-person views of themselves. They look at themselves as they would look at a piece of merchandise and consider, How do I market it? What is interesting about my career? Who is interested in it? How can I get the message out?

You cannot start merchandising yourself too soon, and you should never stop. Making the effort to make positive impressions should be a lifelong habit. Preparing yourself for promotion should be a constant process, not one that kicks in only at annual review time or when an obvious job opening appears. Career breakpoints crop up unpredictably. Even in the best-ordered companies, where personnel planners plot every promotion and transfer months or even years in advance, the human element guarantees that things will go awry. A vice president gets

sick, another drops out to go sailing, and suddenly a
dozen jobs are up for grabs. They will go to those who
have made themselves ready to be promoted.

THE COMPANY VIEWPOINT

Executives in charge of evaluating and promoting employees of major corporations face an awesome task.
There may be tens of thousands of people under their
command. They want to identify and reward the good
ones. They don't want to make mistakes.

And so companies have developed elaborate people-
management systems. At Exxon (according to *Fortune*),
"whenever the presidents of Exxon's 14 regional and
operating companies get together with their principal
subordinates to muse on personnel matters—which they
typically do once a week for about two hours—the hon-
chos have available a so-called replacement table. This
elaborate document lists all the people who report to
them directly, notes when those individuals are likely to
be rotated to other jobs, lists by name the folks likely
to replace them, estimates how long these managers will
be left in their new positions, and sometimes even desig-
nates their successors by name—all this for the next five
years....By virtue of this system, it is possible for management to know pretty clearly which job each executive
will have five, and in some cases ten, years hence."

Other companies go so far as to color-code the personnel records of their employees: green means "promotable," red means "not promotable," yellow means
"maybe."

At the best corporations, a great deal of energy is ex-
pended to ensure, as far as possible, that the worthiest
people are promoted. There is a human tendency to re-

ward loyal supporters with promotions, and office politics is a factor. Wise companies recognize these problems and combat them with impartial evaluation procedures.

"We have a human-resource planning process," says Roger Enrico, president of Pepsi-Cola. "This is separate from the performance appraisals that drive your merit salary increases, and separate from the management-by-objectives that drives your annual bonus. It is something that is done once a year throughout the corporation. Each individual is assessed by his boss as to his strengths and weaknesses and his developmental needs for the long haul, not 'Did he screw up something yesterday?' What does this guy need? What is the sense of how far this person can go? How far do you think this guy can go in the next three to five years? ... And from that, each boss has to develop a specific developmental game plan. It might involve outside training. It might recommend another job experience. Eventually, all this stuff is rolled up. And the president of the corporation goes to every one of the operating divisions and is given a human-resource-planning review, where all the key executives are discussed, and their developmental game plans. From this, he gets a sense of the bench strength, a sense of the talent level, in the organization.

"Also, we have what we call a 'watch list.' It has half a dozen, or a dozen, or two dozen people in various functions in each division who deserve watching. They appear to have tremendous potential. And the list includes what we are going to do with each of these people, and who is assigned to mentor them, to keep an eye on them. ... One of the ways we evaluate our executives is to ask, 'Who have you developed for us lately? Who have you fed to the corporation, to other divisions, to other functions? What stars have you brought in, and brought along?'

"We never have enough talent. We never have enough. You are going to lose some people. People get recruited elsewhere. Some people do not work out. Some people decide to go into business for themselves. And this is a growth corporation. So we usually find, when a big job opens up, there are never four or five candidates. There are always only one or two to pick from."

So Pepsi keeps working on developing, spotting, and labeling talent in its hyperorganized fashion. (So does Korn/Ferry International. So does every other well-run company.) But how does Pepsi, or any other company, define talent? What signs does it look for? Who makes it onto the watch list?

This is how a sampling of chief executive officers describe what they look for in subordinates:

Marshall Manley (Home Insurance): "You promote somebody because of the way they think. Most skills can be learned. But I don't know what's going to happen tomorrow, and I want to make sure that whoever is president of a subsidiary when the unknown happens knows how to think quickly and react appropriately."

Jane Evans (Montgomery Securities): "The ones who are working hard, who are here after hours and are giving the job more than they have to give it."

Harry Gray (United Technologies): "You look at performance, which involves the financial results that an executive gets and his planning for the future. In our business, that means making the correct research decisions. You determine whether the person is a leader. You take a look at his turnover of personnel; that is an indicator of leadership qualities."

Fred Malek (executive vice president, Marriott Corporation): "You have to be able to motivate people. You have to be able to work with people. You could be awfully smart and not have people skills and not do well in our business."

James Harvey (Transamerica): "Of all the qualities a person can have, the best is common sense. Give me a guy with common sense, I don't care if they are an MBA or a CPA or an LLB, and they can react and handle situations. Give me an MBA with no common sense and he's going to be a disaster."

Harvey also says that he looks for courage. When he was a young assistant to former Transamerica chairman

John Beckett, Beckett would sometimes berate him fiercely for the ideas he brought up. "I can remember walking out of his office with my head between my tail and figuring I'd probably better start looking for another job," Harvey recalls. But Harvey would reconsider those ideas and, if he still believed in them, take them back to Beckett and reargue them and sometimes get them accepted. "I learned real quickly that if you didn't have conviction, a guy like Beckett would lose respect for you."

Harvey now applies the same technique to his own subordinates. "I will really challenge somebody. If you came to me with an idea to do something...I might say, 'That's the most harebrained idea I have ever heard of. It is a waste of everybody's time.'" Harvey looks for executives who can stand up to such harsh criticism and will come back and fight for ideas they believe in. "If you are looking for a hard-driven, line-manager type, if you are not going to have to worry about his charging away at stuff or being a Milquetoast, that is the kind of thing you want."

DOING THE JOB

Boil it all down, and the first requisite for getting promoted is clear: do your job, and do it well. And the best way to do that is to help put profits on the bottom line.

Sanford Sigiloff, the turnaround artist who is now chairman of the Wickes Companies, once gave subordinates stiletto-like letter openers embossed with the corporate logo. He explained, "These are either to open your bonus checks or to use instead of coming back here to explain why you didn't qualify for a bonus."

This choice—perform or die—is at the heart of American business. Those who fail to perform may not literally die, but their careers do. Those who do perform build track records their employers—and other potential employers—will admire and reward.

When Albert Snider, former president of Bourns, Inc., first went to work there in 1967, he arrived as director of manufacturing of the instrument division. "I turned it around and made money," he recalls, "and they had seldom made money in the instrument division. Before I got there, they had so much scrap and so much rework that they couldn't get the product out. The people had never felt motivated. I went out on the line, working with the people, seeing they did what needed to be done. I started giving out flowers and pats on the back. We threw all the old dumb products we couldn't make back to engineering. I saw to it that they had more training and did everything I could to increase their motivation. They gobbled it up. People were having fun, and we started going like Grant took Richmond.... All of a sudden Marlon [Bourns, founder of the company] looked at his sheet and came over to see us. He said, 'What the hell is going on over here?' He liked what he saw, and that's when he started moving me, and he never stopped moving me after that."

Snider was promoted, and promoted again, and again, because he made money for the company. There is no great secret about this cause and effect. Fifty-seven percent of the senior executives we surveyed said that "concern for results" enhanced an executive's chances for success. Only integrity rated higher.

Getting results does not come easy, however. Executives who succeed work hard—fifty-six hours a week on average, and many worked longer hours than that early in their careers. They spend an average of ten workweeks a year on the road, compared with only fourteen days of vacation. Asked to name the single factor most responsible for their success, they picked hard work above all else. When Roger Smith, chairman of General Motors, was a young executive at G.M. headquarters on Grand Boulevard in Detroit, a colleague of his told a reporter, "Whatever the senior people wanted done, he did it. In the fifties there was a little joke that if you asked Roger Smith to move the G.M. Building across Grand Boulevard, the only thing he would say was 'Which way do you want it to face?'"

Table 4–1

HOURS WORKED PER WEEK BY SENIOR EXECUTIVES, BY INDUSTRY AND AGE

AGE:	<39	40–49	50>	ALL
Commercial Banking	57.5	53.8	52.6	53.4
Insurance	—	55.8	52.1	53.4
Diversified/Financial	51.7	55.2	55.4	55.6
Industrial	58.3	55.7	54.0	54.8
Transportation	47.5	54.6	53.4	53.7
Retail	—	54.7	54.2	54.4
Other	53.0	56.4	53.2	54.5
Age-Group Average	56.5	55.4	53.7	54.4

Table 4–2

ANNUAL VACATION DAYS, BY AGE AND INDUSTRY

AGE:	<39	40–49	50>	ALL
Commercial Banking	14.8	14.9	15.3	15.4
Insurance	—	14.3	16.5	15.3
Diversified/Financial	5.0	13.6	14.6	13.8
Industrial	10.1	13.9	15.4	14.9
Transportation	12.5	11.1	14.5	13.2
Retail	—	14.2	16.6	15.5
Other	6.2	12.3	14.7	13.5
Group Average	9.7	13.6	15.4	14.6

"Your parents bring you up with the philosophy that if you work hard you will succeed," notes Darryl Hartley-Leonard, president of Hyatt Hotels, "but that is not necessarily always the case. You probably have to reverse it and say, 'If you do not work hard, you probably will *not* succeed.'"

But one should not work blindly or stupidly. If you

slave away for fifteen hours a day, doing the same thing day after day, you are going nowhere. It's not important how long you work; what's important is how hard you concentrate, how *well* you work.

"Anyone who is consistently working eighteen hours a day in the office is not going to get ahead," says William Smithburg, chairman of Quaker Oats (who arrives in his own office shortly after 7 A.M. and leaves about ten hours later). "The person who comes in here at seven o'clock in the morning, and has a sandwich at his desk for lunch, and leaves at ten o'clock at night, all bleary-eyed, with cigarettes all over the place and his desk still a mess, is just plain disorganized. There is a big difference between focusing on minutiae —shuffling papers—and thinking. How in the world can [people like that] think broadly? How can they think creatively if that is the way they spend their time?"

Time is, ultimately, the only asset a person has. Successful executives do not squander it on busywork. They invest it carefully—in both work and recreation. "I have a gym in my house," says Smithburg. "I exercise on the cycling machine and lift weights and so on. It releases the tension. And, you know, I can sit down there on my cycling machine with a little notepad, and things come to mind. I think that is better than just burying yourself in work. I think the quiet and peaceful times are very beneficial."

People who reach the top take advantage of every minute. John Gutfreund, chief executive of Phibro-Salomon, the commodities-trading and securities company, recently told *Fortune* how he reads the newspaper: "I don't have the luxury of reading the obituaries and entertainment sections, or the sports section—which I always used to read first. Now I read the headlines and then go to the financial pages. If I have time, I go into the john at the end of the day to get the other things read."

Another characteristic of those who succeed is that they do what they have to do—*and then they do more.*

When Jane Evans, the former president of Monet Jewelers who is now a general manager in Montgomery Securities, went to work as an assistant shoe buyer for the I. Miller chain in 1965, she recalls, "I did an awful lot of things that weren't required of me. I spent my Saturdays selling on the floor. I'd spend time down in the basement in the receiving room. I was getting in and learning the business from the bottom up."

Where were her fellow assistant buyers while she was doing this?

"They were out on the beach someplace.... The fact that I really got in there and learned was certainly a feather in my cap, and it became apparent that I was going to be an executive a lot sooner than some of my peers." Evans was named president of the I. Miller chain at the age of twenty-five.

People like Evans do outstanding work regardless of external factors. They take responsibility for their own careers and find ways to excel whether the corporate environment around them is supportive of their efforts or not.

"I just had a person in here who's been a marginal performer for the last two years," Norman Blake, chairman of Heller Financial, Inc., said as we began our interview in his office. "He's been rated a four on one-to-five scale, with one being the highest and five meaning you shouldn't be here at all.... I had a long discussion with him, and he made the point that he had not been receiving clear directions from his manager. Over the last two years, he has had poor managers. I was aware of that, but I said to him, 'Look, as far as I'm concerned, having a poor manager who is not giving you good direction is no excuse for not having outstanding performance. There's always something that could be done if you cared enough. If you have enough ingenuity, enough initiative, you can make something happen.' I told him I'd give him six months' probation, and if he doesn't improve, he's out. He has to learn the lesson that he is always his own boss, that he is accountable to himself first. You make the situation; the situation doesn't make you."

GETTING ALONG

When William Waltrip, former president of IU International, was twenty-one years old, he received a remarkable promotion at American Airlines. After only eighteen months in the accounting department there, he was promoted to a supervisory job. He had no accounting education, and no college degree of any kind. He got the promotion, Waltrip explains, "more for what [my boss] perceived my interpersonal skills to be than anything else.... I have always been very cool and calm, and nothing excites me. As a result, I have a good God-given gift to get along with people. [My boss] knew that whoever he put into this job was going to have to get along with ten ladies [in the department], and they were a group of prima donnas." Waltrip's likability got him the job, and gave his career an immediate boost.

Likability is vastly underrated as an element of corporate success. Because a few well-publicized CEOs are certifiable SOBs, some people think being a nice guy is a weakness. I am not talking about being a patsy, however; I am talking about getting along with people in an atmosphere of mutual respect. That kind of likability can carry you a long way.

I have often seen evenly matched candidates go up for a job, with one finally chosen (it seems) at random. What was it about the winning candidate, I inquire, that distinguished him from the equally well-qualified losing candidate? "I don't know," shrugs the person who made the decision. "I just liked the guy."

The importance of being likable is even clearer in the cases of those who do not possess the quality. Some people get fired simply because they are disliked, while a likable mediocrity may coast on in his job for quite a while.

In my own early days at Peat Marwick, I succeeded in part because I liked my boss and he liked me.

"There's one phrase that I hate to see on any executive's evaluation," Lee Iacocca wrote in his autobiography, "no matter how talented he may be, and that's the line: 'He has trouble getting along with people.' To me, that's the kiss of death. 'You've just destroyed the guy,' I always think. 'He can't get along with people? Then he's got a real problem, because that's all we've got around here. No dogs, no apes—only people. And if he can't get along with his peers, what good is he to the company? As an executive, his whole function is to motivate other people. If he can't do that, he's in the wrong place.'"

There is a natural element in likability, of course, but there can be a calculated component as well. It is in your interest to have certain people like you, and you should make the effort to see that they do. (This applies not only to your superiors but also to your peers. Your peers today will someday be your subordinates, if you succeed. It helps to have them on your side.) Approach people openly and honestly. Avoid obvious flattery. Don't make up false common interests. (Don't tell your golf-playing boss how much you love the game if you can't tell a birdie from a 3-wood.) It helps, in getting people to like you, to actually *be* likable.

When Philip Smith, the CEO of General Foods, started his career there as a product manager on instant Maxwell House coffee, he noticed that there was friction between the company's sales and marketing people. "I think all consumer package-goods companies in that time frame went through a power shift from the sales-and-operations area to the marketing area," he says. "There were feelings of losing and feelings of winning, and those can be managed badly by people.... [The marketing people] just felt that [the sales people] had their role, and 'I run this brand, and I am going to tell them what to do.'"

By treating the sales people so brusquely, Smith concluded, the marketing people were hurting themselves. "The sales organization can really make or break a prod-

uct manager by the way they provide support for him....
[And] there is a whole separate reporting relationship
from the sales area up to the general manager that provides a lot of feedback on who the good product managers
are. I wanted to have a reputation with the sales organization as someone who really understood the business,
rather than as some graduate-school expert. So I went to
them and said, 'Look, I don't know anything about this
business. Tell me the half-dozen best sales managers we
have in the field and help me schedule some time with
each of them.' I went out and worked with all these guys,
so they could tell me what they knew about the business.
This helped me, but it also made me them feel differently
about me.... They felt I had a lot of respect for them and
their importance to the business."

Needless to say, this did Smith no harm.

William Smithburg, chairman of Quaker Oats, also
mended fences with sales people at a crucial point in his
career. His first job at the company was as brand manager
for Aunt Jemima frozen waffles, a product he soon realized had been put into national distribution before an adequate supply had been arranged. "I was supposed to be
marketing manager and every day my total task was to sit
down and figure out which truck goes to what customer.
They were screaming and yelling about not having
enough waffles." Smithburg proposed that the product be
withdrawn from the southern region until a second manufacturing plant could be built, and his plan was approved, despite some concern about what would happen
to the southern-region sales force while they had no waffles to sell. "Once the decision was made, they all accepted it," Smithburg says, "...[but] I went out of my
way to get to know the guy who was in charge of the
southern region. I said, 'I am really sorry for this, but you
have to understand that it is in your best interest. What
we would like you to do now is work the eastern region
for two years, and then we will take you back in the
South.' I tried not to make it as though I had won some
battle with the guy." Two years later, Aunt Jemima fro-

zen waffles returned to the South and were a big success. And Smithburg had made a friend of the man he had temporarily put out of a job.

Such elemental human relations cost very little, and can only help smooth one's way to the top.

SERVING THE COMMUNITY (AND YOURSELF)

The résumés of chief executives are interesting documents. That of Larry Horner, chairman of KPMG Peat Marwick, is especially revealing. It has two lines of text under the heading "Education," six lines under "Business"—and thirty-three lines under "Civic."

In New York, where Horner has lived since 1984, he is either a member of the board or an officer of the Tri-State United Way, the New York City Partnership, the Lincoln Center Institute, the Metropolitan Museum of Art business committee, the Governor's Council on Fiscal and Economic Priorities, the University of Kansas Alumni Association, and other organizations. In Los Angeles (where Horner lived for seven years), he is or was a board member or officer of the California Chamber of Commerce, Loyola Marymount University, the Los Angeles United Way, the L.A. Music Center, the Museum of Contemporary Art, the Orthopaedic Hospital, and the California Economic Development Corporation. In Miami (where he worked for three years), he is or was active in the Dade County Vocational Education Foundation, the Greater Miami Free Trade Zone, the University of Miami, the Lowe Art Museum, the Philharmonic, the opera, the chamber of commerce, the South Florida Council of Boy Scouts, and more.

Horner is active in civic organizations to an unusual degree (they once held a Larry Horner Day for him in Miami), but it is a rare successful executive who does not serve the community at all. Active participation in charitable, political, social, and cultural groups is today a necessary step on the ladder to the top of the business world.

Such activities serve several purposes. First and foremost, they do good, and I strongly believe in giving something back to society. Second, they provide a necessary escape valve from one's office life. "It makes you a better executive to have a broad view of the world," says Roger Enrico of Pepsico, who is on the boards of the New York City Opera and two colleges. Finally, and most practically, they are a very effective form of networking. While serving the community, one makes important peer-level contacts. It is often very difficult to make a cold call to a senior executive at a potential client company and arrange a get-acquainted meeting; if you are working with that executive on the mayor's finance committee, you are *already* acquainted.

"In our profession," says Larry Horner, "we are very lucky in that if you are active in your community, it fits together with a valid business purpose. You meet people, potentially gain more clients, and have a chance to see your client executives in a nonworking environment and therefore have a better relationship. I've always felt very strongly that if you're lucky enough to make a good living, you should give something back to your community....I am lucky that that fits together well with our efforts in marketing and client service."

It does not matter which civic groups you choose to join. Politics is fine. So are religious groups, or anything else that interests you. The point is to get involved, and to be perceived as being involved. This serves not only the interests of your company, but your own. "I was quite active in the Kansas City community as a relatively young man," says Horner, "and I probably progressed more rapidly because of that, because I would wander into opportunities where I could influence an individual to become a client of our firm." Horner attributes his election as chairman of Peat Marwick partly to his partners' awareness of his "extracurricular" activities. In situations where several candidates with similar records are competing for a promotion, one's civic involvement is often the weight that tips the scale.

You are never too young to get involved in civic activities. If you are at an early stage of your career, and you are doing your volunteer work with people who are also young, they are likely to be people who will be very important in their companies five or ten years downstream. Wherever you are in your career, however, try to get involved in your civic work at the highest level possible. There is no point in being a worker bee, stuffing envelopes, when you can be on the board of directors. And that's often not hard to arrange; civic groups are always desperate for people willing to assume responsible positions.

The only problem here is that you may have a hard time getting yourself turned on to do these things. You might prefer to stay home and watch a football game. As a matter of fact, so would I. But you simply do not have that luxury, not if you are marching to the drum of success.

STRATEGIC MOVES: GETTING . TO THE POWER CENTER

If you are doing your job well, your excellent performance will count the most if you are performing where important people can see you. Throughout their careers, successful executives gravitate toward centers of power, and the exposure they get there contributes to their success.

This applies at all levels of the corporate pyramid. If

your career is just beginning, and anything above the division level seems irrelevant to you, then you want to be near the head of the division; don't worry about anything else. If you are an excellent mid-career finance person, you want to be on the staff at corporate headquarters, not that of an unimportant subsidiary. When Donald Regan switched from being secretary of the treasury to become Ronald Reagan's chief of staff, he explained that the White House was a sort of "corporate headquarters," and that was where he wanted to be. There are both mini and maxi centers of power. The center at your level (or one level up) is where you want to be.

Ray Hay, the chairman of LTV, had achieved a high position at Xerox—president of the company's domestic copier business—when Xerox moved its headquarters from Rochester, New York, to Stamford, Connecticut. "They moved corporate finance and corporate planning and corporate marketing to Connecticut," Hay recalls, "and I was left in Rochester, running what was called the Business Products Group, which was really the domestic copier group. And I was not quite sure what had happened. I was kind of a division manager, and the corporation had moved away. In a lot of ways, I felt good about that. I was glad to get all those guys out of my hair, because I really liked my job. I was running the domestic copier business—the manufacturing operations, the engineering, product design, quality control, marketing, sales, advertising. I really liked that.

"After I was there for a while, Peter McCullough [then Xerox president] called me down to Stamford, and he said, 'Ray, we would like you to move to Connecticut and be executive vice president.' And I said, 'What would I be running?' He said, 'Well, the Business Products Group would report to you,' and a couple of other things. It was not clear to me exactly what-all would report to me. I would leave the job I had, and *that* would report to me. But I would be in Connecticut rather than Rochester. And I said, 'I don't know, Peter, if I want to make that move or not. I really like this job I have.' And he said,

'Well, that is up to you. But of course, if you do not make this move down to corporate, you can't ever be president.'"

Hay got the message. He moved to Connecticut. Although he was ultimately a runner-up for the president's job, his move was essential to his strong candidacy.

"Generally speaking," says Hay, "you've got to be clearly visible to the power structure, and you've got to be visible in a way that can cast a good light on you. People who are not known do not tend to get promoted."

Hay notes that this does not *always* require being at the power center; sometimes being there can actually be counterproductive. "It depends on the organization. People might tend to think that they know all of your warts and problems if you are up close, whereas you look a lot better if you are farther away, *if your results are good.*"

This is what happened to Peter Ueberroth when he was a very young man. In his early twenties, he worked in Hawaii for Trans International Airlines, which was owned by the financier Kirk Kerkorian. A vice president's job opened up at headquarters in Los Angeles, and the two leading candidates were a man in the L.A. office and Ueberroth. "There is a problem in business in this country," says Ueberroth, "where if you look at somebody in a position every day, it's hard to think of him in [some other] position. But if they don't see you every day, if you're off somewhere, they say, 'He's pretty good.' They really should have taken the man in Los Angeles, but they didn't. They went and got me from Hawaii [for the vice president's job]."

(Kerkorian, by the way, evaluates the situation differently. "He [Ueberroth] was quite young," Kerkorian recalls, "but he was very impressive, very mature for his age, very aggressive in a nice way. He shot ahead of guys in their forties. I was impressed by his maturity and his ability to handle people.")

Trans International Airlines was a small operation in those days. Even though Ueberroth was thousands of miles from corporate headquarters, he was still clearly visible to people there. In a situation like that, it can be beneficial to be away from the power center. In a larger organization, where visibility is obscured by distance, it is a riskier proposition.

Getting to the power center may sometimes be accomplished simply by asking for a transfer. Not all young executives will have the foresight to plan their careers around the power-center strategy. Those who see its value may be able to get there just by requesting the assignment. This may entail some initial sacrifice on an executive's part, such as moving oneself and one's family to a distant city, or accepting a job of lower rank than one could have elsewhere. But the power center is where things happen and where, in the long run, all top executives reside.

WORKING ABROAD

Nothing can be farther from the corporate power center than a foreign country; yet overseas assignments, if certain risks are provided for, can be valuable building blocks to a successful career.

There is no question that the more experience American business people have abroad, the better off American business will be. American companies today are players in a global marketplace, and not always winning ones. American economic dominance is being challenged where it was once unquestioned. Even at home, foreign products are aggressively attacking established American industries. In response, American companies are sourcing overseas, entering into foreign joint ventures, and devising new international strategies. To meet these challenges, we need a new generation of internationally oriented business leaders, preferably with foreign job experience, foreign-language proficiency, and familiarity with cultures other than our own.

So international assignments are good for the country and good for the company; but are they good for you?

In one important respect—money—they certainly are. International executives reported the highest average income—$286,000—in our executive survey. They were considerably ahead of the second-place group (general managers, at $264,000) and the overall average ($235,000).

Nevertheless, many executives are reluctant to go abroad. They are afraid of being away from headquarters for long periods of time, afraid such absences will have detrimental effects on their corporate power bases. But these nervous executives are overlooking something important: in an overseas management position, a competent executive can often achieve dramatic results, and get noticed for them, more quickly and more spectacularly than in the United States.

Early in his career, Roger Enrico, today the president of Pepsi-Cola, was working in marketing at Pepsi's Frito-Lay snack-food subsidiary when he was offered the opportunity to run Frito-Lay/Japan. "That was a very small business, about five million dollars a year in sales, and an unsuccessful business at that, one in which we had been losing a lot of money," Enrico says. "I was a marketing director [at Frito-Lay] and had damned near two-thirds of the business and ninety percent of the profits under my marketing responsibilities." Nevertheless, he took the Japanese assignment. "A lot of people thought I was crazy, going off from a meteoric rise at Frito-Lay and jumping onto this tangent over in Japan. My feeling was that it was time for me to expand my knowledge base beyond brand management—dropping coupons and working on advertising campaigns—to run something, albeit something small, and to run something in an environment that was new. I thought, 'No matter what happens, I will gain a tremendous amount from this experience, whether the business becomes successful or not, whether I get lost in Tokyo from Pepsico's standpoint or not.'"

But Enrico did not get lost in Tokyo, primarily because, in moving to a smaller subsidiary abroad, he had picked up the crucial title of general manager. "If you are a general manager, you are going to get more of the attention of the top management of the corporation than if you are a functional guy. Decisions have to be made, about little divisions as well as big divisions, that must go to senior management." Enrico decided that the best thing for Frito-Lay/Japan to do was sell half of itself to a Japanese food company. He entered into negotiations, and "people like [Pepsico Chairman Donald] Kendall and Andy Pearson, who was president at that time, had to get involved. They had to sign the contracts. So I got visibility right at the top."

Larry Horner, chairman of Peat Marwick, also benefited from this paradoxical visibility-at-a-distance when he was assigned to the accounting firm's troubled German operation midway through his career. "By being dumped into a very new, very strange foreign environment, with no command of the language, and being able to turn it around and make it economically viable, I think that proved something beyond what I'd proved when I was part of the Kansas City office.... and I think it helped me tremendously."

These are the advantages one finds abroad: valuable international experience, the chance to be a big fish in a small operation, and the attention of top management. But going abroad can still be risky, if the company that sends you has no tradition of and procedures for reintegrating foreign assignees back into U.S. operations.

At enlightened companies, this is no problem. Richard Braddock, sector executive for consumer banking at Citicorp, spent three years in London without worrying about vanishing over the Citicorp horizon. "It was in my perception not a risk because Citicorp has a truly well-developed international culture. Many of the senior managers, if not most of them, worked abroad at one time or another in their careers."

When the time comes to consider a foreign move in your own company, look at its record. What happened to people who were sent overseas four years ago? Have they been heard from since? Are they happily back at work at good jobs at home? Will the company make a commitment to you about the length of your tour abroad and the type of job you will get when you return?

If the answers are positive (but only if they are positive), go.

AVOIDING THE STAFF SYNDROME

We at Korn/Ferry recently conducted a search for the president of a $250-million division of a major corporation. The corporate chairman met with us as we prepared to begin, and he threw out the name of a particular top executive in a competing company. The chairman had met this fellow and been impressed by him; he asked us to take a look at his background.

When we did, the man was eliminated from consideration. He was intelligent, and successful, and every bit as impressive an individual as the chairman had thought— but he had never had profit-and-loss responsibility. He was a chief financial officer and had spent his entire career in financial staff positions. Years before, he should have been given—or asked for—a division to run. Because that had never happened, we had no choice but to rule him out of consideration for the president's job. He was a chief financial officer, and he would be a chief financial officer for life.

To reach the top of an American corporation, you should, at some point in your career, get profit-center responsibility. You must put profits on the bottom line. If you make money for a company, the company will notice, and so will headhunters.

The difference between staff and line positions is basic. Staff people—in finance, accounting, public relations, law, personnel, engineering, and elsewhere—do essential work in corporations, but they are not responsible for nor do they contribute directly to the bottom line. They do not make money; they spend it. (And most of them don't understand the distinction.) Line executives, on the other hand, supervise and weave together the work of staff people in pursuit of the corporate lifeblood—profits.

Now, many fine careers are built on the staff side. People who rise to the post of chief financial officer or chief counsel make important contributions to their companies and do very well for themselves. (And some do become CEOs.) But most careful strategists of their own careers make a point of getting out of staff positions before they become staff lifers, because they know there is a definite limit to how high staffers can rise. "A lot of people grow up in corporate organizations through an area of expertise," says Ray Hay, chairman of LTV, "and they become really proficient at their jobs. So, in the end, they become the chief functional officer of some kind. But once you are the chief functional officer, where else is there to go except to be the president? Yet being the president is an altogether different kind of job than being a chief functional officer."

The senior executives we surveyed, therefore, took part in a sort of mass migration from staff to line jobs during the course of their careers. Only 3.7 percent began their careers in general management; 43.8 percent are in general management today. As their numbers in general management grew, their representation in staff areas shrank correspondingly.

Star performers like Jane Hurd, who became chief executive officer of the Children's Hospital of Los Angeles at the age of thirty-four, exemplify this trend. When she was twenty-nine, Hurd was executive assistant to the chief of Los Angeles County's department of health and hospitals. "That was like the highest-paid staff job in the world," she recalls, "and it had a great deal of reflected responsi-

Table 4–3

PERCENTAGE OF SENIOR EXECUTIVES IN VARIOUS JOB FUNCTIONS

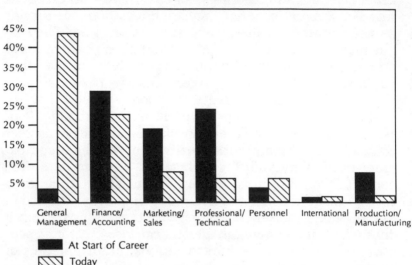

■ At Start of Career
▨ Today

bility and authority. I was running the internal organization for the director and working with the Board of Supervisors, the governing body of the county. They had a meeting every Tuesday, and every Tuesday there would be five to ten health-related items on the agenda. I had to make sure, behind the scenes, that the votes were all lined up and all of the problems ironed out, so that there were no surprises for my boss. It was a very challenging job.

"But my boss said to me, when he pulled me up out of the organization to be his executive assistant, 'You only want to do this for about eighteen months. Because this is not where the real action is. The real action is in line operations. So I want you to do this for a while while you are preparing yourself to be a hospital administrator.'

"After a while, he came to me and said, 'It is time for you to move into a management job.' And he arranged for me to spend some time working at County Medical, which is a big medical center, to get some experience on my résumé."

From there Hurd got an appointment as associate administrator at another county hospital. Her next post was chief administrator of Harbor-UCLA Medical Center, yet another county hospital. And from there, a mere four years after her first line job, Korn/Ferry recruited her for the top position at the prestigious (and privately run) Children's Hospital. Hurd's well-plotted move from staff to line positions had succeeded perfectly.

Donald Beall, the CEO of Rockwell, altered his career in response to the same kind of advice Hurd received. Beall is proud of having been the youngest divisional controller Ford ever had, yet he took to heart some advice from an early mentor. "He told me not to stay in finance too long, but to run something." When Beall was hired away from Ford by Rockwell, he worked out an understanding with his new employer. "I would spend a year at the corporate office, helping them set up their financial planning [a staff position], but what I really wanted to do was get into line management. And so, just about one year later, I was moved to Rockwell's electronics business as the number-two guy. They took a gamble [and so did Beall]." Neither Beall nor Rockwell ever looked back. His appointment to the presidency was announced before he turned forty.

Other top executives made similar moves. Norman Blake spent part of his General Electric career in public relations. It was a very exciting time (the late 1960s), and Blake found himself negotiating with unions for their endorsement of the SST supersonic-jet program, working with state governors on plant closings and openings, sponsoring "rap sessions" with students protesting General Electric's role as a weapons producer. It was interesting and fun; but Blake got worried.

"The public relations experience was a good one to have, but it didn't lead anywhere. I looked at my peers, and their average age was probably fifty. These were nice jobs that were given to loyal, hardworking middle-management employees; they were almost like a retirement slot. And here I was, in my early thirties, saying, 'My

God, is this what I have to look forward to for the rest of my life?' "

Blake got out.

John Chamberlin, who scrambled to move from light-bulb sales into an internal consulting group when he was at G.E. because that was the hot place to be, later fought even harder to get *out* of the consulting group. "When you take a staff job," he says, "it's always a risk. My agreement was I'd be there only two years. It actually lasted three years. At the end of the third year, I told them I wanted to go. They said, 'No, we want to keep you a fourth year.' I said, 'I'm not going to stay a fourth year.' As far as I was concerned, I had learned about all I was going to learn."

G.E. stood firm, so Chamberlin actually went out and got a job with another company. Only after he gave notice did G.E. relent and transfer him. "I didn't want to get locked into being a staff man," Chamberlin explains. "There's a period you can do that. But you stay there too long, and you're there forever."

It may not be appropriate to move to a line position until you are midway in your own career; but to succeed, you ought to be aware of the need to make such a move from your first day on your first job, just as you ought to be thinking about positioning yourself at corporate power centers or in highly visible posts abroad. Meanwhile, at all points in your career, you ought to be making friends, working in the community, and above all, performing excellently. These steps are not in themselves guaranteed to propel you across the $100,000-a-year barrier, but they *will* make your big career moves come that much easier.

PART 5

MOVING UP: PLOTTING YOUR CAREER

MOST PEOPLE work at their jobs in a state of anxious ignorance. At every stage of their careers, they worry about how they are doing. Does the company consider them to be performing their duties well? What exactly does the company consider their duties to *be*? What is the likely future course of their careers?

On these and other crucial questions, there is often an implicit conspiracy of silence. Bosses, as a rule, are terribly uncomfortable about evaluating their subordinates. It makes them nervous. It sometimes involves delivering bad news. It raises awkward questions of personality. They don't know what to say. So they often do everything they can to avoid saying anything at all.

Subordinates, for their part, are fearful of discovering what their bosses really think of them. They don't want to know how they are doing because, deep down, they are afraid they aren't doing very well. So they do not ask. They wait to be told. And they can wait their lives away.

HOW ARE YOU DOING? (DARE TO FIND OUT)

You cannot hope to succeed in business unless you pierce this conspiracy of silence. You must realize that you will not harm yourself by discovering how you are rated. Even if the news is bad, you will be far better off knowing it than not knowing it.

Without this information, good or bad, you cannot possibly plan your career in an intelligent way. Too often, executives make bad career decisions out of ignorance. They may be very highly regarded in their companies, but because no one has bothered to tell them, they worry themselves into unhappiness and accept less promising jobs elsewhere. Conversely, they may make the mistake of remaining for years in dead-end jobs, declining better offers elsewhere, because they are under the mistaken impression that their employers are grooming them for greater things.

One simple indicator of how well you are doing at your job is whether or not you like it. And one way to determine *that* is to consider whether you like getting up in the morning and going to work. If you have to drag yourself out of bed, you probably like your job less than you think you do, and you may very well be in trouble there.

Another simple indicator: do you like your boss? If you like him, he probably likes you. If he likes you, that's probably *why* you like him, whether you realize it or not. If you don't like your boss, it's another warning sign; the feeling is likely to be mutual.

THE MOST VALUABLE THIRTY MINUTES OF THE YEAR

Most companies attempt to deal with the problem of employee evaluations by conducting formal reviews at least once a year. Every employee is summoned individually for a session with his or her boss, which may involve the preparation of a written evaluation form and the presentation of that form to the employee.

These annual sessions have the potential to be the most valuable thirty minutes of the year for employees, yet most of these meetings do not fulfill their promise, and many are outright disasters. Executives don't like reviewing other executives, so they tend to conduct the sessions hurriedly and superficially. Subordinates are uncomfortable as well, so after a few minutes of stiff conversation about performance, talk may turn to the Super Bowl.

Even the heart of the session is likely to be filled with meaningless buzzwords, which is the easy way out for both participants. One's boss may say, "You are doing just fine," or "We think you have a very bright future here," or "I really like the way you handle yourself," and then hand over an 8-percent raise. The employee leaves feeling fine, and the evaluation is over, to everyone's relief, until the following year.

If your boss evaluates you with phrases like that, ask yourself, "What have I really learned?"

This is what you *should* learn:

1. Was a written appraisal made of my work?
2. If so, can I see it?
3. How, exactly, do I rank among my peers?
4. If I got a raise, was it based on my performance, or only inflation? How does it compare with other raises?
5. What are the general growth opportunities within this company?
6. Am I considered promotable?
7. If so, when am I likely to be promoted? What job am I likely to be promoted to?
8. If not, is there anything I can do to make myself promotable?

You should ask all these questions, and make sure you get answers to them, at least once a year. If your company has formal evaluation sessions, take advantage of those. If it does not, you may have to trip your boss on the way to the water cooler. Whatever it takes, do it.

Some of these questions are admittedly blunt. One way to ease into them is to ask where your boss thinks you may be in your career two years from now. (You might also ask where *he* expects to be in two years; that can be a clue to your own progress.)

There is probably no subtle way of asking how you rank among your peers, but it is something you need to know. If there are four people at your level, and you are number three, you will have to decide if you want to be following one and two up through the ranks forever, or if you would rather move to another division or even another company.

ARE YOU PROMOTABLE?

The key thing to keep in mind in any discussion of your job performance is the difference between the questions "How am I doing?" and "Am I promotable?" New York mayor Ed Koch made a trademark of asking people on the street, "How am I doing?" The answer in most cases was "Just fine, Ed." Then (in 1982) Koch ran for governor and failed. He was doing just fine (as mayor), but the voters did not consider him promotable to governor.

The same thing can happen in your own career. You may be doing great in your current job, but unless you want to do it forever, the crucial question for you is whether you are considered promotable. Asked directly, your boss may try to avoid answering directly, but in his evasion you may learn something. He might ask you to consider whether you really want to be promoted, whether you really want all the pressures of a bigger job, whether you aren't really content where you are. The more he fudges, the less promotable you are. (If he does come right out and say you're not considered promotable, then you are on the job market. Face it.)

Many people are afraid to raise this question, because

they fear the answer will be negative. But you should ask anyway, despite your fears. It is better to hear bad news than to be ignorant of it. If you are not considered promotable, you may discover that it is because of circumstances beyond your control (the division is scaling back), or that it is because of circumstances *within* your control (you haven't taken enough initiative in your current job, or you don't know enough about interest-rate swaps). If it's the latter, you may be able to take action to improve your performance and make yourself promotable by the time of your next evaluation. Even in a worst case—the company considers you irrevocably at a dead end—knowing that will enable you to start planning to move. The situation is still not hopeless. It is hopeless only if you don't know about it.

IS YOUR NEXT JOB THE RIGHT JOB?

If you *are* promotable to the next job up the corporate ladder, and it is clear you are going to get it, your planning should not end there. It is time to consider whether that job is the job you should be seeking.

Remember, there is a difference between having good jobs and having a good career. The next obvious job on the ladder for you may be a fine job, but it may not be an effective step toward your ultimate goal. It may even be a mistake for you to take it.

Consider the splendid career of Richard Braddock, who is today immensely successful as head of Citicorp's enormous consumer-banking division. In 1973, Braddock was a twenty-nine-year-old marketing and development manager at General Foods. He was doing very well there. "I had been in a series of marketing jobs of growing responsibility throughout the company," Braddock says. "And I moved, I think, as well as anyone through General Foods." More promotions were obviously in store, so Braddock took stock of his situation, measured it against his goals, and did the logical thing.

He quit.

That decision was rooted in Braddock's clear sense of what he wanted to achieve in his career. "I was doing fine," he says, "but as I approached my thirtieth birthday I began to think more broadly about what I wanted to be as a businessman." His medium-term goal, he decided, was "to have, by my mid-thirties, a rounded set of experiences that would qualify me to run a medium-sized company of some sort. I felt that if I had some solid marketing skills, some good financial skills, and some demonstrated ability in managing large numbers of people, I would have a set of components that would at least in theory qualify me to run something."

So Braddock made his list:

1. marketing experience
2. financial experience
3. people-management experience.

It was clear that he could check off number one. He had worked at General Foods since finishing graduate school, and all his time there had been spent in marketing. "After nine years of it," he says, "I was probably as good at it, or as bad, as I was going to be."

That left numbers two and three. Braddock considered: was there any chance of getting them if he stayed at General Foods? "I felt that if I stayed there," he decided, "I would face a series of further marketing jobs of growing magnitude and responsibility, but which were not fundamentally different from what I'd done before." He might have managed to switch into the finance area, but "the financial department at General Foods in those days was looked on as a second-class citizen." More important, he had doubts about the direction and vitality of the company. "It was a pretty big, unwieldy, and relatively unaggressive place in those days," he says.

Just as Braddock decided to leave, a job offer arrived from Pepsico. "There were some interesting elements to what they were proposing, but it was not fundamentally different from the General Foods experience." It did not meet Braddock's criteria of offering financial and people-management experience. It was a good job, but Braddock passed.

And then came Citicorp, which was just then beginning what became a major revitalization of its consumer-banking area. The company was seeking a marketing or merchandising executive for a job that would once have gone automatically to a career banker. The offer to Braddock was this: come in for a short tour as assistant to an executive vice president and then take over responsibility for all Citibank branches in Long Island, the Bronx, and Westchester.

As a career move, this held out risks. There was as yet no tradition of marketing people moving to banking. "I'm sure it was viewed as a heretical act," says Braddock.

But the job offered precisely what Braddock was seeking. The branches employed seven hundred people; there was his management experience. Citibank was a bank; there was the finance. Braddock took the job.

His road to the top from that point was neither assured nor clear. He found the culture of banking a greater change from what he knew than he had expected. ("I had to keep a little book in my desk explaining what an interest rate was," he recalls, with mild exaggeration.) And he expected, in fact, to stay at Citicorp for perhaps five years, en route to his goal of running a (nonbanking) company.

Things worked out differently, as things will. Braddock is happy and fulfilled today, running Citicorp's consumer-banking division. This was not where he expected to find himself fourteen years after leaving General Foods, but his landing there was made possible by his defining, in 1973, precisely what he wanted from his career and then deliberately moving to get it by walking away from the promotions he did not want and putting himself instead where he needed to be to learn what he needed to learn.

JOBS AS LEARNING
EXPERIENCES

Some of the best careers are crafted by those who use their early working years to gain diversified on-the-job business educations. In selecting jobs and assignments, these individuals accord prestige, titles, and even compensation less consideration than opportunities for learning. The diverse experience they acquire is especially valuable today, when business is more complex than ever before and competition for top positions is intense. A breadth of knowledge and experience gained by what may appear to be a rambling series of jobs can pay off big in later years.

"I think the greatest inhibitor to people's true career development is the notion that somehow there is a career path, some linear sort of thing, that you go from step to step in some sort of connect-the-dots line. That is crazy," says Roger Enrico, president of Pepsi-Cola, whose own career has included stints in Pepsi-Cola bottling and running Frito-Lay operations in Japan and South America. "The best thing you can have is a zigzag type of career path [within one company], a zigzag series of experiences."

In 1986, when *Fortune* named Norman Blake, the chairman of Heller International, as one of "America's most wanted managers," it noted that he had made nineteen career moves in twenty years. As is the case with most successful executives, Blake made most of his moves within a single company (in Blake's case, General Electric, where he worked for fifteen years). Even so, he managed to zigzag a great deal. He worked in computer sales and computer product planning, in public relations

and computer time-sharing operations, in strategic planning for industrial equipment and the management of international joint ventures. Many of the job moves he
made—including many he actively sought—were lateral,
with no increase in rank or pay.

"As a philosophy," he says, "I never ever talked about
salary or grade or anything. I always went after the experience. I didn't want to scare away the opportunity by negotiating for money.... I've moved nineteen times, or
whatever it is, and each time I perceived a real opportunity to learn something and broaden my skill and experience base so I would have broader options in terms of my
own career growth."

Blake had no specific objective in mind at the start of
his career beyond knowing that he wanted "to manage
people and to manage large organizations," an ambition
he has now fulfilled at Heller, a three-thousand-employee
finance company owned by Japan's Fuji Bank. "There's no
question I've been lucky," he says, "but I also like to
think that I really prepared myself for opportunity by the
variety of diverse experiences I had."

Blake tackled enough different learning experiences to
qualify himself for any one of half a dozen successful careers. He was well prepared for almost any kind of opportunity that might have come knocking.

Other ambitious executives, particularly those who
have already achieved some success, are more specific in
the kind of experiences they seek.

The lifelong ambition of Gary Wilson, now executive
vice president of the Walt Disney Company, has been to
be a chief executive officer, yet he worked for many years
at the Marriott Corporation, where he concluded that he
had no chance of ever becoming CEO.

"I was going to leave Marriott long before I did because
I'd added all the value I could, I thought," Wilson says.

(Note Wilson's interesting use of language. One "adds
value" to a product. The product here is both the Marriott
Corporation *and* Gary Wilson, potential chief executive.)

"But every time, [Marriott Chairman] Bill Marriott

would offer me something I needed and wanted. In 1981, I wanted to go someplace where I could be a CEO. Bill Marriott knew that, but he just couldn't deliver on that, not unless he died or decided he was going to go off and do something different. But he did offer me the opportunity to punch my ticket from an operations point of view by taking over Marriott's in-flight catering business.... At some point, when you're coming up on the staff side of the business, whether it be marketing or finance, you have to get some operating experience. And that's where the risk can be tremendous. If you fail in your first operating job, maybe for reasons that are beyond your control —the market's bad, the gasoline crunch, whatever—that can set you back for a decade in trying to achieve your goal.

"Bill Marriott gave me the opportunity to punch that operating ticket, yet keep all the rest of my portfolio [as the company's chief financial officer] so that if I failed it wouldn't be a big black mark on my record.... We had long talks about what I wanted to do, and this was his response to keep me happy. It was a good response. He was very clever about that."

Wilson did a fine job with the in-flight catering business and stayed at Marriott for three years longer than he otherwise would have. Marriott was happy to have him, and Wilson was happy to gain the kind of experience he knew he needed to eventually become a CEO.

THE ZIGZAG PATH

Some progressive companies today are so convinced that broad experience bases produce the best executives that they are prodding their promising employees to do some zigzagging, whether they want to or not.

"We have been spending a lot of time here convincing our people that a straight-line career path is not good for them," says Roger Enrico of Pepsico. "'Career path' are the worst two words ever invented to describe a way to get ahead, because they imply some sort of narrow, programmed thing.

"We do not have a lot of formalized training. Our belief is to move people from function to function. You don't do this with everyone, but with the high-talent people, the ones who appear that they really have something going for them. We move them from division to division and let job experience be the training ground.

"We'll take a young marketing person and say, 'Look, do you know what you ought to do right now, while you are young and have the chance? You ought to go out in the field and spend a year in sales.' He'll say, 'Why would I want to do that?' We'll explain, 'Because that is where the rubber meets the road. And you will learn how we really make money, and the details of running the business out there. And you will never forget it. It is kind of like boot camp—maybe you won't like it while you're doing it—but it will give you a perspective on things that will really do you well in the years ahead.'

"And he may say, 'Well, I don't know. I'll get behind my peers here. While I'm gone out there, someone might get promoted to brand manager, and it won't be me.'"

But such worries, Enrico says, are shortsighted. "He would not be forgotten. He would come back. And my view is that when he comes back, he might come back into a brand-manager job. And his peer might have been promoted a year earlier, but he is going to go right past the guy, because he got that perspective, and the other guy did not."

Pepsico's program of encouraging such transfers has already had some successes, Enrico says.

"A young lady was the brand manager of Slice. She was terrific. She had a huge amount of potential. And no way did I want to see her move on, even though she had been running that brand for two years. For the business, I wanted her to stay. But you have to do right developmentally for the person. She had learned all that she was going to learn.

"She came into my office, and I'm sure she had a sense that I was going to find some way to enhance her, or promote her, or add more stuff to her.... And she said, 'I just wanted you to know that I know that you care about what I'm doing. And I know that you want to see me leapfrog ahead. But I want to go work as a bottler. I want you to get me a job with our New York bottler, and I want to do that for a couple of years.'

"I said, 'Why do you want to switch?'

"She said, 'I want to learn how the business really operates on the street.' We ended up sending her to our company-owned bottling plants in New Jersey, where she is the marketing director for the East Coast....

"I took a guy who was a vice president in one of the marketing functions, who had spent all his time in brand management. He is a very bright guy, about thirty-five years old. His wife is a doctor, and she got pregnant, and they had a baby, and, boom, we had a wonderful window of opportunity, because now they were mobile. She had left doctoring for a couple of years. So I called him in and said, 'I want to move you to San Francisco, where I am going to put you into our division sales manager's job for the western division.' Now, that is technically a demotion. He was already in a higher pay grade. So I said, 'We will "red circle" you, so that your status and compensation stay with you. The reason I want to do this for you is you will never get another chance. And you need to get out and see the real world and run something.'

"He loved the idea. It is a developmental assignment. He is betting that he will do well, well enough that he won't lose his visibility. And he will probably be back here in a big job sooner than either of us thinks."

Pepsico has now done this kind of thing enough, Enrico says, and enough people are aware of his own nonlinear career path that "that starts to become the [corporate] culture.... People say, 'Well, that must be *the* career path, zigzagged as it is.' And now people want to do it. And that is what you want. You want them to want to do it."

WHITHER GOEST THOU?

The idea of seeking out lateral career moves—or even, as in the case of the vice president who went to San Francisco, technical *demotions*—may take some getting used to.

"You cannot imagine how many young marketing people I have talked to about moving from one job to another who just said no," says William Smithburg, chairman of Quaker Oats, another company that encourages promising young executives to get at least a little experience outside the marketing area that is the traditional path to the top there. The company has managed to move some people around. Some promising middle-level managers have accepted plant or overseas assignments, Smithburg reports, and when they return, they tend to do well.

Enough rising stars have now had successful temporary tours away from corporate headquarters that, Smithburg says, "all of a sudden people are beginning to see that it is a positive. And now we are finding people knocking on our doors, saying, 'Gee, maybe you want me to go to Fisher-Price [a toy company owned by Quaker Oats].'"

But not all companies are so conscientious about moving employees around for their own good. It is each employee's responsibility, in any case, to decide which jobs will best lead him toward his chosen career goals. The easiest job to get—the next job on the ladder—may not always be the one most worth having.

Making intelligent choices about one's next job requires knowing several things:

- What does the company think of you? Are you considered promotable? If so, what is your next job likely to be?
- What are your career goals? Will your likely next job lead you toward them?
- If not, where can you position yourself to gain the experiences you need to have?

Answering those questions, and acting on the answers, are the essence of successful career planning.

PART 6

BREAKING OUT

I N EVERY successful career, there is at least one turning point, a moment when opportunity presents itself. The alert and ambitious executive watches for this moment, this window of opportunity, and he seizes it. It is his chance to break out from the pack of his peers.

There is a general consensus among senior managers as to both the existence of the breakout phenomenon and the time when it occurs. Only 4 percent of those we surveyed said they had broken out before the age of twenty-six. Only 12 percent said they had broken out after the age of forty. The largest number broke out between the ages of thirty-one and thirty-five. This coincides with the average age (thirty-four) at which the largest number broke the $100,000 barrier.

There are, of course, some notable exceptions to this trend, managers who suddenly surge ahead when they are well into middle age. Far more common, however, are

Table 6–1

AGE AT CAREER BREAKOUT

AGE	PERCENTAGE
25 or less	4.2
26–30	24.5
31–35	34.5
36–40	24.4
41–45	9.1
46–50	2.9
Over 50	0.4
	100.0

those who fail to break out by the age of forty and then never do. If you are not on the track to success by your late thirties—if you have not begun to move out by then from the pack of your peers—then you had better get going (unless you are planning on working until you are 105).

One reason many people fail to break out is that they simply do not want to. They are regional sales supervisors, or public relations directors, or assistant divisional controllers, and they like their jobs and their lives just the way they are. They enjoy their work, and they are grateful for their paychecks, and while they might *wish* for more, they do not *want* more badly enough to do anything to get it. By the age of thirty-five, their lives are set. They can see clear to the horizon, and they feel just fine about that.

Those who would succeed are fundamentally different. If they are well settled in their jobs and can handle them easily, they are not content; they are bored. David Norman was a successful corporate president when boredom led him to quit his job and found the Businessland chain of computer stores. "It just wasn't quite as exciting as it used to be to jump out of bed at five thirty in the morning," he explained to *Fortune.*

Those bound for success are never content to spend their years idling in that realm of the corporate hierarchy called "middle management," which I defy anyone to define, other than to say it is what one should get out of. For the ambitious, middle management is the place of no place. It is the place to pause while positioning oneself to move up.

Fortunately, corporate promotion patterns are more flexible today than they used to be. You no longer have to go from a $40,000 job to a $45,000 job to a $50,000 job. With the proper planning, you can leapfrog levels. You can break out.

THE CROWN PRINCE GROUP

The easiest way to break out is never to have to, because you are *already* ahead of the pack. This is the circumstance of the "fast-trackers," the boy and girl wonders who seem to have been *born* halfway up the corporate ladder.

A few of them were, of course. The right connections, the right schools, the right parents gave them substantial head starts. But most thirty-five-year-old vice presidents owe their early success to what they have made of their lives, not what they inherited. They simply set themselves to the task of succeeding earlier than most people.

Often the first successes of such people are entrepreneurial ventures they conceive themselves and labor at tirelessly, even while they are full-time undergraduate or business students. Such first successes almost invariably lead to second successes. I know that if I were hiring graduates straight out of business school these days, I would go after the ones who are running the vending machines, the laundry services, the little newspaper-distribution companies.

Success is a habit that it pays to develop young. Not only does it give one the direct material rewards of one's achievements, but it also gives one the feeling of being successful. This feeling shows, and it is attractive to bosses and prospective employers. The sooner you *appear* to be successful, the sooner you *will* be.

If you have not founded Apple Computer by the time you are twenty-five, however, do not despair. There are still steps to be taken that can put you on the fast track. A good MBA from a prestigious school, for one thing, can get you into a high-level training program in a good company. (This is, in fact, what MBAs are *for*, in addition to the education.)

Once on the job, you ought to deliberately strive to become a superstar as early in your career as possible. This might mean working eighteen hours a day; often, at the early stages of a career, it is simply hard work that distinguishes one employee from another. Your time will be especially well spent if you devote part of it to something beyond your assigned duties. Find a task that will appeal to your boss, and to your boss's boss. Often this is something that your boss would or should be doing himself if he had the time. Present it to him all completed, in such a form that he can take credit for it but his boss will know that you also were somehow involved. Everybody will be happy, and you will have been noticed.

Another strategy, which is for some people a temperamental necessity, is to eliminate a lot of climbing up the corporate ladder by starting at, or near, the top. Some people do well by investigating job opportunities in small, offbeat, and growing companies. "My patience level is rather low," says Paul Montrone, president of The Henley Group, an industrial conglomerate. "Climbing up the rungs of a corporate ladder was not something that ever appealed to me. I preferred to avoid that process by going into smaller companies, even if that meant assuming more risk."

And so Montrone (who, in his college days, had run a laundry service and a tutoring service) avoided major corporate jobs after earning a PhD from Columbia's business school. His first civilian job, after a stint in the Pentagon, was assistant to the chairman of a cement company. Montrone was twenty-six. Within a year, he was chief financial officer of a start-up high-technology company, where he was thrown into the middle of major financings and reorganizations. "I cast about to try to wind up being where the action was," Montrone says. "I acquired much of the knowledge I needed by OJT—on-the-job training. . . . Instead of going and burying myself in a staff job [at a large company], I elected to join smaller firms at a level where I had decision-making influence, even at a very young age."

The enduring advantage of getting ahead of your peers early in life is that once you are ahead, all you have to do to stay ahead is move at a normal pace. William Waltrip, who became president of Pan American World Airways at the age of forty-four, made his first break out of the pack especially early. After eighteen months in the accounting department of American Airlines (where he had been hired with no college degree), he was promoted—"at the ripe young age of twenty-one," he says—to a supervisory position. "I will never forget it. I had ten women reporting to me, five of whom were over fifty. And they were a big help to me, because I think they wanted to see me succeed." From that point on, as he moved toward the presidency of Pan American, Waltrip was always the youngest of his peers, by far, in every position he achieved.

GAINING VISIBILITY

If you are not already a star, how do you become one? The answer is twofold:

1. Do good work.
2. Make sure people know about it.

Note that both halves of this formula are crucial. You can be doing the greatest work in the world, but if your boss doesn't know what you're doing, and your boss's boss doesn't know what you're doing, then you are dead. You might as well just take your money home every two weeks and be happy. You're not going anywhere.

On this, senior executives agree. Almost two-thirds of those we surveyed said visibility was of significant importance *or greater* to an individual's chances of succeeding.

At Korn/Ferry International, we have a policy of flying

Table 6–2

**IMPORTANCE OF VISIBILITY AS A FACTOR IN SUCCESS
AS RATED BY SENIOR EXECUTIVES**

Least Important	2.3%
Limited Importance	6.9
Moderate Importance	27.5
Significant Importance	48.3
Most Important	15.0
	100.0%

short distances in coach class, to save our clients money. A while ago, one of my associates suggested that we stop doing this, because our clients didn't know about it and so did not appreciate it. I said, "No, that is wrong. We shouldn't switch to first class. What we should do is make sure our clients know we are flying coach." There is no sense in just being a good soldier, unless it brings you absolutely enormous satisfaction. If you are doing something that benefits somebody, let him know about it.

Visibility is important for executives of every rank, from those in entry-level jobs to those in the top fifteen corporate slots. It is especially important for members of the crowded baby-boom generation. There are a limited number of spaces at the top of our major corporations, and baby-boomers have little hope of gaining one if the people who already occupy those spots do not know that they exist. Norman Blake had worked at General Electric for years, and had done excellent work there for years, before what he describes as a "decisive moment in my career." He got a job as a strategic planner in G.E.'s plastics division, where one of his superiors was Jack Welch. "I was able to get into Jack Welch's business, and I got exposed to Jack Welch, and I was able to demonstrate my capabilities to a guy who was really a rising star." Welch shot up to become G.E.'s chairman. Blake rose to the executive vice presidency of General Electric Credit before leaving to become CEO of Heller Financial.

Of course, it certainly helps to have something positive to show off when the opportunity to be seen presents itself. Sometimes that thing can be as simple as being a hard worker. Every chief executive officer I know works weekends. And what would warm such a person's heart more than knowing that some of the people he has high hopes for in the organization are also working on weekends? He would never come right out and ask the question Did you work Saturday? But, if you *did* work Saturday, find a way to make sure people at the top know about it.

Other achievements speak for themselves. When Ray Hay began his career at Xerox (where he rose to executive vice president), he was one of many office sales managers. He broke out of the pack and made a name for himself by tackling a chronic, unresolved problem.

"The service part of the business was the biggest problem Xerox had initially," Hay recalls. "There really was no system. The service organization was pretty much run by dispatchers, and that was the low end of the business.

"The whole concept of Xerox had been predicated on a brilliant move, to go forward on a rental rather than a sales basis. And so we had the first real service-oriented business in the office-equipment industry. But it depended upon service, because once people got these copiers, and these copiers became an integral part of their businesses, they really needed to have those machines working. And since we had a really new technology with xerography, and very sophisticated machinery, product downtime was a major problem for a lot of offices. Yet we were so busy selling this new product, and expanding and growing, that nobody paid very much attention to service.

"When I came into the New York office, sales was not a problem. We were renting out the machines as fast as we could hire salesmen to go out and take the orders. But everybody was suffering from the problems of the service organization. So I turned my attention there. I created service territories, and dispatching systems, and all of the things that would tend to make that end of the business more dependable. As a result, people [in other offices] started looking to us to find what we were doing, because we were dealing with the service problem.... The opportunity was there to shine. And there was not a whole lot of cloud layer to hide it."

At General Foods, Philip Smith, who became CEO, stood out as a young brand manager by using the specialized knowledge he had brought with him from his previous job in advertising. "I used that to gain some distinction for myself," Smith says. "I developed a training program in advertising for my group, which other people looked at, saw the benefits of, and wanted to copy. So I developed a reputation for being good at advertising. I picked that area because, first of all, I *was* good at advertising, and, second, most of the people who had come to General Foods straight out of school were better at other fundamental business things than I was. They knew more about production and promotion. But I knew advertising, so I used that to advantage."

In 1956, in the Ford organization, a young assistant sales manager named Lee Iacocca made a name for himself with a bright idea. "While sales of 1956 Fords were poor everywhere," he wrote in his autobiography, "our district was the weakest in the entire country.... I decided that any customer who bought a new 1956 Ford should be able to do so for a modest down payment of 20 percent, followed by three years of monthly payments of $56. This was a payment schedule that almost anyone could afford, and I hoped that it would stimulate sales in our district. I called my idea '56 for '56.'... Within a period of only three months, the Philadelphia district moved from last place in the country all the way to first. In Dearborn, Robert S. McNamara, vice-president in charge of the Ford Division, ... admired the plan so much that he made it part of the company's national marketing strategy.... And so, after ten years of preparation, I became an overnight success."

My own early career got a crucial boost because of a piece of work I did for Del Webb, the big real estate developer, when I was a management consultant with Peat Marwick. Webb was only my second client, and he handed me a tough problem. (In fact, I had lobbied for the assignment; I knew it could be important to me.) All of a sudden, banks were asking Webb for his personal guarantee on loans being made to his real estate company, and he wanted to know why. After forty-eight hours of nonstop work, I could see that Webb's real estate operations were going to lose a considerable amount of money that year. This had not been obvious to everyone, because Webb's managers had been doing some "creative" (but legal) cost accounting, pre-planning profits and transferring costs from closed jobs to open jobs in order to meet their profit goals. I told Webb that, and the losses subsequently materialized. Webb said, "I knew it was happening. I just did not know how." Webb was so pleased with the work that Peat Marwick got him as a major client, and that made my career. I became a star at the age of twenty-six.

I accomplished this partly by applying the second half of the formula for visibility: If you do good work, make sure that people know about it. Nothing is gained by being shy, and I was not. Webb offered, and I encouraged him, to let senior partners of Peat Marwick and executives of other corporations know how pleased he was with my performance.

Of course, there has to be a little subtlety in this kind of thing. Some restraint must be employed in the means by which one broadcasts one's successes. (Do not rent a bullhorn.) A young man I know edits an internal newsletter for the top management of a major brokerage firm. He is deluged with suggestions from individuals in the organization that he include items about their latest projects. His newsletter is an easy and elegant pathway to visibility at the highest levels. So my friend is a very popular fellow around the office—he is constantly wined and dined by people with editorial "suggestions"—and no wonder. (Is there an appropriate internal newsletter in *your* organization? Can *you* get mentioned in it?)

Another means of gaining recognition for your good works lies in the subtle art of using the carbon copy on reports and memos you prepare. The two people you have most to be concerned about at every stage of your career are your boss and your boss's boss. When you have done something great, and you are reporting to your boss about it, it is an excellent idea to "cc" a copy of that report to your boss's boss. The only possible downside of such a maneuver is that your boss might demand, "Why did you do that?" It shouldn't be too hard to come up with a plausible reason for informing your boss's boss of your achievement. In a pinch, ask your boss, "Oh, do you mean that you did *not* want me to send it to so-and-so?" The only answer is obvious: "No, it's fine."

Your objective here, however, should not be to antagonize your boss. (In most cases, he or she won't mind anyway.) If he does mind—and you know that he might—it is still worth crossing him if you have had a truly shining moment; the news should go out. A better strategy in many cases (depending upon your relationship with your boss and the nature of your company) is to contrive to share credit for what you have done with your boss. Or let your boss get the credit for the job, with just a hint—but a clear one—that you were somehow involved with it.

Whatever you do, do not deluge your boss's boss with junk. Broadcasting news of unimpressive performance will only hasten your demise.

For some employees, unfortunately, the hope of gaining visibility is remote. They are at such a junior level or in such a crowded organization that it may be almost impossible to do something especially impressive in their work. If you are in a "cookie-mold" job, where you are doing the same work as many other people, and there are many other people who could stand in for you, your job simply may not lend itself to the kind of marginal contribution that can win you notice. If you are, for example, one of five hundred lending officers in a huge New York bank, and anyone who has had any banking training could walk in and take over your duties at the drop of a hat, and you are in no position to generate significant new business or do anything innovative, you have got to ask yourself a few hard questions:

1. Should you move to a small bank in Rhode Island? Working in a smaller organization may be your only chance to do something that will be valued. Everyone, in fact, should consider the opportunities available in small companies from the time he seeks his first job. In a small company, everybody is visible all the time, and sizable responsibilities are often given to young employees. "You can show a lot more in a small firm than you can in a big firm," says Gary Wilson, executive vice president of the Walt Disney Company, who started his own career in a small consulting firm and prospered there. "Of course, if you're bad, you bomb out a lot faster, too." (The down side of this strategy is that overall, large companies offer more opportunities than small ones, simply because they offer more jobs. Gary Wilson himself, a brilliant executive, eventually worked at two large and well-admired corporations, Marriott and Disney.)

2. Is there anyplace else you can go that will heighten your visibility?

When William Waltrip was in his third airline accounting job (with Frontier) at the age of twenty-five, it was one of his responsibilities to work on industry committees that were designing a new system of airline ticketing for travel agents. "When we finally got the travel agents to stand still for the program," Waltrip recalls, "there had to be an organization put together to implement the plan. The president of the Air Transport Association asked me to come to Washington to go to work for the Association and perform that function. I saw this as a great opportunity for exposure to everybody in the business. . . . I spent three years there, and I put the program in place, and I developed, as a result, an industry-wide reputation. I was known by everybody in the business." Once the new system was running smoothly, Waltrip (naturally) got bored with running it. But the visibility he had achieved soon led him to another challenge, and a bigger job, at Eastern Airlines.

3. If you are already employed in a large company, and want to stay there, is there any way to gain attention internally that is not directly related to your job performance?

When William Glavin, the vice chairman of Xerox, was a young salesman for the IBM-owned Service Bureau Corporation, he was asked by the dean of the business school he had attended (Wharton) to join a committee that was setting up an alumni organization. "So we wrote the by-laws," says Glavin, "and had our first annual meeting. We decided the way to get the organization started was to pick an 'Honorary Alumnus.' We put down some criteria and went out and asked for candidates among our alumni.

"I nominated the man who happened to be the president of the Service Bureau Corporation, who was really a young star in the IBM organization. . . . And he won, and came down and spent a day with us at Wharton, where he went to classes, and met the dean, and so on. We had a dinner that evening and honored him with a plaque. I was his host the whole time. Within a few weeks, there was an opening [for a sales manager] in Dallas, and I got the job. I got that opportunity because of my association with Wharton. I don't know if I was recommended by the president for the job; he was four levels above me. But here I was, a twenty-four-year-old guy right out of school, and they moved me to be a manager in Texas. . . . Getting promoted to manager at twenty-four was very unusual in those days. It got me ahead of everybody else." (In addition to this stratagem, Glavin was doubtless helped by the fact that he was brighter than most in his peer group.)

4. Can you give a speech?

Call the program chairman of a trade association with an upcoming meeting. Tell him that you want to speak. If you do get booked, keep your mouth shut about it until the last minute, so that nobody else preempts you. As the speech date approaches, go to your boss for formal permission, if your company policy requires it. (The memo

requesting permission is a perfect example of one to carbon to your boss's boss.) Write: "I have been invited to
speak to the Widget Trade Association next month.
[Don't say you invited yourself.] The subject is why our
company's widget-rotation policy is the greatest in the industry. I would like you to be aware of this. Carbon copy
to boss's boss." Then march into your boss's office and
say, "Is it okay if I interview you for what I am going to
say in my speech?" Your boss will say, "Sure." Then say,
"Great; can I also talk to your boss?"

When you give the speech, your boss will know about
it; your boss's boss will know about it; your peer group
will be green with envy. I don't want to imply that this is
all gamesmanship, but believe me, if you don't do it,
somebody else will.

An alternative to giving a speech is writing an article
for the trade press. Talk about something you are doing in
your company as a case study.

Better yet, have an article written about you. This is,
admittedly, largely outside your control, but, if it happens, the results can be terrific. When *Fortune* ran an article headlined "America's Most Wanted Managers"
about a group of businessmen whom "executive
recruiters...covet most as future chief executives," the
stock of those listed soared. "I referred the article to the
executive-compensation committee," joked Douglas
McCorkindale, the vice chairman of Gannett, who ranked
in the magazine's top ten.

5. Can you climb the Empire State Building?
This is not entirely a facetious suggestion. It is not un-
common in big organizations to find large numbers of
people doing similar jobs similarly well. Even if you do
one or two outstanding things *in addition* to your core
duties, it is likely that many of your peers will have done
one or two different but equally outstanding extra things
on the job. The only way to truly distinguish yourself
may be to seek achievements outside the office. An outstanding athletic accomplishment is one possibility (win
the local marathon or pro-am golf tournament). A more

feasible one for most people is to gain a position of promi-
nence in a worthy community organization. (It doesn't
matter if the group is charitable, religious, social, or political.) It isn't hard to gain a responsible position within
such groups; they always need help. Wherever you get
involved, however, make sure that you are *perceived* as
being involved. This will reflect well on your employer,
and that, in your employer's eyes, will reflect well on
you.

TAKE A RISK

One consistent thread running through the careers of executives who have successfully broken out is that they
were not afraid to take risks. They spoke out, they
changed jobs, they argued with bosses, they tackled assignments with uncertain prospects for success. They
demonstrated, almost without exception, that they would
rather be challenged and at risk than safe but bored. And
it paid off.

It is a good idea to take on as much risk as you can
early in your career. Succeeding in risky situations identifies potential leaders more clearly than anything else can.
You may have less to lose than you think, and a great deal
to gain.

Fully one-third of the senior executives we surveyed reported that the breakthrough that put them on the path
to success involved "taking on a high-risk project." Other
elements that ranked high as breakthrough components
—changing jobs, working on new products and projects—
also often involve substantial risk. Yet these executives
all made it to the top.

Many people entering the business world today have
not learned this lesson. "Our most significant talent pool

Table 6–3

FACTORS INVOLVED IN CAREER TURNING POINT

FACTOR	PERCENTAGE
Right Place, Right Time	49.7
Different Functional Responsibility	46.1
High-Risk Project	33.4
Switching Companies	31.5
Launching New-Product Project	16.1
Aligning with Right People	12.5
Lateral Move	9.6
Other	8.0

in the company is the bright young MBAs that we hire," says William Smithburg, chairman of Quaker Oats. "They are very well paid from the day they walk in the door. Here are these bright young people with this tremendous future. They've spent all this money on education. They've made strategic decisions in doing their cases in school. Yet a number of them do not succeed in our organization. The reason is that they are too risk-averse. They behave in an almost lockstep fashion. They do not stand out from the crowd. So few will stand up and say, 'I believe the business I am responsible for here should be run differently....'

"The point is, you *can* be an innovator. You *can* be a risk-taker, and almost entrepreneurial, in a large corporation. We *want* to spend more money. We have strong cash flows. We want projects to develop. We want more things to do. Yet we find people can become very short-term oriented. They can become near-term numbers oriented. They don't have the vision. They don't have the willingness to take risks.

"Now, it is a fact of life that, as a publicly held company, we have to live by quarterly and annual reports.... We have a series of financial targets [that] are translated down to the lower managers as a plan. The plan becomes numbers, and as a general rule, you have to make your numbers. You have to have financial success. And so people say, 'Wait a minute. If I go out and use an added five million dollars for an innovative new promotion campaign for Cap'n Crunch in the third quarter, I may risk missing my numbers.' My reply to that person is 'Now you know what life is all about. If you *don't* come up with new ideas and take some risks, I can assure you you won't get ahead. Because you will not stand out....' The biggest risk of all is to take no risks. If you never take a risk, you will do nothing. You will stand still. And the world will pass you by."

Those who take risks possess self-confidence, and self-confidence is indeed a general trait of most successful executives. "You've got to have enough confidence in yourself that you're not worried about being fired for saying or doing the wrong thing," says William Glavin of Xerox. "You cannot let anything scare you. If you really have confidence that you can always get another job, then you will do the right things."

One of the most successful executives we interviewed tells a story of how his confident attitude led him to confront the chairman of his company when he was just a young mid-level employee:

"This guy scared the hell out of everyone. I would sit outside his office and see people waiting to go in and see him. They'd go into the bathroom and get sick first. I mean, he was that kind of guy.

"I was asked to do an assignment for him, so I made a study, and I went in with my boss to see him with a presentation and recommendations. I put my charts up and I started to say, 'Here is what you asked me to do, and here is how I went about it, and here is what our recommendation is.' And he said, 'I don't buy that recommendation.' I said, 'Well, let me have a couple of minutes and I'll explain to you why.' So I started flipping the charts. I got through the first chart, and he said, 'That doesn't tell me anything. Let me tell you why you are wrong.' And he went through this whole litany of why my recommendation was wrong. He hadn't listened to anything I said, because I hadn't had a chance to say anything. This was all in the first four minutes. And I said, 'I don't think you and I are working from the same base of facts. What I ought to do is take you through this and then you will understand that.' He said, 'Okay.' I flipped the next chart, and he said, 'I don't agree with that either,' and went off on his tirade again. I flipped the charts back over, took them off the wall and rolled them up. He said, 'Where are you going, young man?' I said, 'You already know what you want to do. I am trying to tell you you are wrong, and you won't even listen. I've got a different set of facts than you've got. I did the work; you didn't.' He said, 'Put that thing back up there and finish.' So I put it back up and began to go through it, and the same thing happened thirty seconds later. I rolled the charts up, put them under my arm, and said, 'There is no sense in my wasting your time. You run a big corporation here. You know what you want to do. Fine, we'll do it.'

"My boss couldn't believe what I was saying, because he was one of the ones who played the game all the time. The chairman said, 'Young man, are you telling me that you won't let me tell you what I think?' I said, 'No. You told me, and I accept it. I think it is wrong, but I accept it. You are the boss, not me.' He said, 'You put your charts back up there and go through them.' I looked him right in the eye, and I said, 'I'll do that under one condition; that you don't say another word until I'm finished.' He said, 'Go ahead.'

"It took fifteen minutes. I went through it and walked out of the office, and my boss said to me, 'That was the worst demonstration I have ever seen.' The chairman called me in the next day and said to me, 'I want to tell you something. I didn't like the way you handled yourself yesterday, but you were right in the end. I agree with you now.' And from that day on we were buddies. My philosophy of 'Call it as you see it' has always paid off."

Now, this particular executive took an enormous gamble. His confidence that he could always find another job may well have been put to the test. I certainly do

not recommend that young managers deliberately antagonize their superiors. But there is definitely something
to be said for taking a stand. His own mentor, William
Smithburg of Quaker Oats says, taught him to make
aggressive recommendations. "He said, 'Don't come into
a meeting just to chitchat. Come into that meeting
with a point of view. Don't come in waiting to see
where your boss is going to lean.' I have seen a lot of
that. I see a lot of that right now." Smithburg admits
that his perspective has been altered now that he is at
the top himself. But he still retains his impatience with
"fencesitters."

"Someone once said that having a point of view is
worth fifty IQ points," says Roger Enrico, president of
Pepsi-Cola. "One of the things we look for when we are
assessing people on their way up is 'Do they have a point
of view?' Do they have the guts to recommend what
might be unpopular solutions to things?"

Enrico's own career took a couple of unusual twists because, like Glavin, he believes one should not worry too
much about keeping one's job. "Everybody controls their
own career," he says. Take note of that. It is absolutely
true and at the core of my own beliefs.

"The company never controls your career," Enrico says,
"because you always have one big option, which is to
leave the company. You can always go somewhere
else....I was still pretty young when I figured out that
my family was not going to starve to death. I knew how
to earn a living. I wasn't worried about whether I could
pay the electric bill."

With this confidence, Enrico made the risky job change
described in Part 4, leaving his position as marketing director at Pepsi's Frito-Lay subsidiary for an uncertain assignment as president of Frito-Lay/Japan.

Enrico's corporate colleagues thought he was crazy to
make the move, including "a fellow at Frito-Lay who was
my peer, the other marketing director. He said to me, 'I
just cannot believe you are doing this. This is the greatest
thing that ever happened to me. Because now I am a

shoo-in for vice president for marketing, an absolute shoo-in.'

"But I didn't worry about it. I figured if Pepsico did not view my performance in Japan as being adequate to want me in further positions Stateside, either because of 'out of sight, out of mind' or because of true lack of performance, then what the hell? I wasn't going to starve. I would have gone someplace else. I mean, why worry about it? Why sit there and sweat all of these things that might happen to you? If you do that, you will never do anything. And then nothing will happen to you."

Once established in Japan, Enrico decided the best course for the company there was to enter into a joint venture with a Japanese firm, a move which required the approval and attention of top Pepsico officials. "The conventional wisdom was against entering joint ventures. So I had to change people's minds. And, in the process of doing that, you get a chance to demonstrate that you have a point of view, which is pretty damned important, instead of just reporting on things."

The joint venture was approved. And as a result of the visibility Enrico gained in advocating and negotiating it, he was promoted to run a much larger Pepsico subsidiary in South America. "Andy Pearson, the president of Pepsico, who had gotten involved in some of the decisions [concerning the joint venture], must have sensed, 'Look, this guy seems like he has some potential. He has enough guts to make decisions and operate on his own.'"

And what about Enrico's peer back at Frito-Lay, who had been elated at Enrico's departure for foreign parts?

"The ironic thing was he never did get the vice-president-for-marketing job. I went away for three years. When I came back, he was gone. And I came back as vice president for marketing."

There are, of course, risks and risks. In moving to Japan and advocating a joint venture once he got there, Enrico had not gone hog wild. His joint-venture recommendation followed an in-depth study he commissioned from an outside consultant. "I didn't pull this out of my hat. We did a lot of homework before we came to these conclusions." Similarly, Enrico's belief that the Japanese experience would be beneficial regardless of the success of the business there and his optimism that he could find another job if worse came to worst were far from unreasonable. The risks Enrico took were, in sum, prudent.

"It's clear," says Donald Marron, the chairman of Paine Webber, "that among the people who do the best today are the ones who retain an entrepreneurial risk-oriented perspective but are very disciplined. If you think of your scope of business activity as an ever-widening circle with you at its center, then the stronger you are at the core of that circle, the more risk you can take at its perimeter. For example, if you're going to be a very successful trader, you need the best possible technical understanding of your products; you need a disciplined strategy in trading your markets; you need the best computer support available; you need a thorough understanding of your clients. When all those fundamentals are solid, you can take a risk at the margin. It may look like a big risk, but it is founded in this great core of understanding and support."

With this kind of groundwork underlying many of the risks taken by successful executives, those "risks" were often a lot less risky than they appeared to the successful executives' less confident peers. Some were, in fact, "win-win" situations.

In the late 1950s, for example, John Chamberlin (former president of Avon) was still at General Electric, where he eagerly accepted an assignment to develop a marketing plan for a new electronic tape system that would produce "instant movies."

"It was risky," Chamberlin says, because there was no guarantee that the product, which was still in development, would ever work. "As it turned out, I worked on the plan for a year, and then we found out that the tape didn't work. . . . It just didn't work. We couldn't get anything out of it."

But Chamberlin came out ahead anyway. During his year on the project, he had several opportunities to present his plan to top G.E. brass. "I made presentations to the president of the General Electric Company....I was able to show a lot of people how I thought, how I could put things together, how I could present things." After the instant-movie project was junked, Chamberlin was promoted to a good job in G.E.'s television division. (The television sets worked.) He had been involved in a losing project, but Chamberlin had emerged a winner.

THE TURNAROUND

If, as Chamberlin's career demonstrates, one can benefit by being associated with a division that fails, imagine how much more one can gain by being involved with a failing division that is resurrected. Some of the most dramatic career breakouts result from turnaround situations, where an executive takes a chance, signs on with a lackluster venture, and turns it into a roaring success.

Perhaps the best-known turnaround of recent years is that of the Los Angeles Olympic Organizing Committee. When my partners Dick Ferry and Norm Roberts persuaded Peter Ueberroth to leave the prosperous travel business he had founded to head the LAOOC in 1979, the future of the entire Olympic movement was in doubt, and the Los Angeles committee's assets consisted of a cardboard box of files and $300,000 in debts. Ueberroth's achievement in creating the fabulously successful 1984 Games from that cardboard box earned him the well-deserved admiration of millions of people and made him the most sought-after businessman in the country. (Today, of course, he is commissioner of baseball.)

Executives who have engineered less publicized turnarounds have become just as popular within their own companies. After Larry Horner, now the chairman of Peat Marwick, revived the accounting firm's troubled German operation in the early 1970s, he was given his choice of moving to several American offices, including the one in Miami, which was having problems. "There were a couple of opportunities, and I talked to the chairman about them. I told him I preferred Miami because it seemed to be more challenging. I think he chose me to go there because I'd been in a difficult situation before."

Horner succeeded in Miami as he had in Germany. "It became fairly apparent that [turning around difficult situations] was something I was skilled at. And it gave me a fair amount of recognition. Also, I enjoyed it. You know, you can see something happen. It's a lot different than taking on an office that's rocking along and doing well."

His desire to face challenges, and his success at meeting them, drove Horner to the top. His partners recognized his ability and achievements by electing him chairman in 1984. Even then, he did not cool down. In an audacious move that stunned the accounting profession, he proceeded to engineer the merger of Peat Marwick with KMG Main Hurdman. Before the merger, Peat Marwick had been the nation's second-largest accounting firm. Today, it is number one.

"The real opportunity for me," recalls William Smithburg of Quaker Oats, "came in 1971." That was when Smithburg was made general manager of the company's cereals division, which was, he says, in the midst of "very bad times.... The ready-to-eat-cereals business was not making money. Commodity prices had skyrocketed, and there were Nixon price controls, so our margins shrank. It took a lot of conviction and persuasiveness on my part and on the part of the people I worked with to sell management on continuing to support these businesses.... That was a very big decision for the company in those days. There were people who felt the numbers weren't good enough, that we shouldn't invest in it. There was even talk of closing one of the cereals plants. I and others pleaded, 'Don't! Wait out price controls. Wait out the grain problem.'"

Smithburg and his crew devised a number of new strategies and tactics for the cereals division. Some were as simple as making the biscuits in Life cereal less fragile. "They were breaking up, and the last bowl you got was crumbs, and that's the one you remember, so you don't buy another box." Others required substantial investments in advertising and promotion. "We had Cap'n Crunch, and Life, and 100% Natural Cereal, which were terrific brands, but it took a marketing effort. It took the right television commercials. Do you remember Mikey? We made the decision to invest the dollars behind the Mikey advertising. That was part of the strategy for Life, to say the product tastes good *first, then* it's good for you. We did that strategy on Life, and another one on Cap'n Crunch, and another one on 100% Natural Cereal. We started to put money into them, and management went along with what I recommended. It was gutsy in its day, and risky. I'm sure that had it been a big failure, I would certainly not be *here* [in the chairman's office] today."

In 1971, when Rockwell International first invested in the Collins Radio Company (which Rockwell ultimately acquired), Donald Beall, then a relatively new Rockwell employee, moved over to become executive vice president of Collins. "Collins was virtually bankrupt when we did the deal," he recalls. "Collins had incredible strengths in avionics, telecommunications equipment, transmission, and switching...but they had gotten into some other areas that they should not have. They had the economy working against them, and things were very bleak.... So you might say that it was somewhat of a risk; but I had a great deal of confidence that they were in the right markets and had the right market position."

What would the effect have been on Beall's career if Collins had collapsed? (In addition to being involved in running it, he had been among those who urged Rockwell to buy it.)

"That would have been a big black mark," says Beall, who is today Rockwell's CEO. But Collins prospered and so, as a result, did Beall.

FIND A NICHE

Sometimes the way to break out does not involve doing something better; it involves doing something that is not being done at all. Many successful executives began to move up the corporate ladder when they stopped trying to outdo their peers in their assigned responsibilities. They accepted that *everybody* was doing his or her job well, and that it would be difficult to do one's job so much better than one's peers that one would stand out from the pack. So (while continuing to do their own jobs well), they looked for something *else* that needed to be done.

This tactic was employed by Harry Gray, chairman of United Technologies, when he first went to work for a then-new company called Litton Industries in the early 1950s. "I'd learned a couple of things," Gray says. "One is that in a growing situation, you want to find a niche which keeps you visible to the top management. I went into Litton in commercial market planning. Fine. I could do that.... Then, from being near the headquarters, I saw one other opportunity. That was that they really didn't have anybody handling their public affairs or their affairs with Wall Street except Tex [Thornton] himself. There were a lot of guys who wanted to talk to [Litton co-founders] Thornton and Roy Ash, but Thornton and Ash only had a limited amount of time. There were guys backing up [who wanted to talk to someone], so I just volunteered. I said, 'Tex, let me talk to them. I know the story.' So he did let me talk to them. And the next thing I knew I was handling their public affairs." Gray did not stay in public affairs very long, but by moving into that niche, he had made a strong impression on the people at the top.

Gary Wilson, at a middle stage of his career, was chief financial officer of Marriott and was responsible as well for the company's real estate development program. "We developed one billion dollars' worth of hotels a year, so that was by far the most important thing I did." And how had he been assigned this crucial corporate role? He hadn't. He had found a vacant niche and moved into it. "Part of the strategic plan in 1975–76 was that we were going to expand the hotel business, and to expand the hotel business you had to build hotels. So I started. I just did it. Nobody else knew how to do it. I didn't either, but I did it." Bill Marriott encouraged him, and Wilson and the company thrived.

My own career, back when I worked as a management consultant at Peat Marwick, advanced twice when I moved into newly created niches there. When the firm entered the field of executive recruiting, I jumped at the chance to open its western search division. Several years later, I helped persuade the firm to expand into the area of organizational consulting and then moved into that area myself, breaking out of the pack of traditional consultants. In both cases, the new field was wide open. There was plenty of room to grow and be noticed. Until I cofounded Korn/Ferry International, they were the best career moves I ever made.

DO MENTORS HELP?

The most important thing to know about mentors is what they cannot do. A mentor cannot make his protégé a success if his protégé is not capable of becoming a success on his own. What a mentor can do is help that protégé get an opportunity to show his stuff.

Or *her* stuff. In recent years, women in the corporate

work force have looked a great deal to mentors to help them gain their bearings in unfamiliar territory. This is not at all surprising, because that is the other thing mentors are good for. Mentors know the ropes, and so they are useful to people new to the corporate world. In recent years, that category has been loaded with women, but it also contains all new corporate employees of both sexes.

The senior executives in our survey found mentors useful. Almost three-quarters said mentors were of at least moderate importance to an individual's chances for success:

Table 6—4

**IMPORTANCE OF MENTORS AS A FACTOR IN SUCCESS
AS RATED BY SENIOR EXECUTIVES, BY AGE**

| | AGE GROUP | | | |
	<39	40–49	50>	all
Least Important	—	5.4%	7.8%	6.8%
Limited Importance	30.4%	17.1	19.9	19.1
Moderate Importance	30.4	38.6	37.5	37.8
Significant Importance	30.4	30.5	26.5	28.0
Most Important	8.8	8.4	8.3	8.3
	100.0%	100.0%	100.0%	100.0%

Mentors are especially important early in one's career, when they can impart basic information about the corporate culture and serve as role models for moving through the corporate environment. How they dress, whom they deal with, what they *do* are actually more important to the education of observant protégés than anything their mentors *say* to them. Most successful executives have a series of mentors, adopting new ones as they reach each new level on the path toward the top. Former mentors are likely to remain friends, even as they become subordinates.

When the time arrives to break out, however, there is a severe limitation on what a mentor can do. Career breakthroughs are the rewards of achievement. No mentor can achieve anything for his or her protégé. The best he can do is guide that protégé to a position where achievement is possible.

FIRST AMONG EQUALS

As I moved up at Peat Marwick, heading toward becoming a partner at the youngest possible age, some members of my peer group began to envy and dislike me. This was inevitable. The corporate world is a pyramid. As you climb that pyramid, people who have been your peers will begin to disappear from your level. The playing field contracts, while the number of players does not. Those left behind are not likely to be happy about it, nor will your passage upward endear you to them.

We begin competing with our peers in childhood. In school, we compete for the best grades. Later, we compete for the best jobs. By the time we start competing for raises and promotions, rivalry has become a way of life.

The savvy competitor keeps close track of his or her standing in the pack. In the course of your annual job evaluation—or any other time or way you can get the information—find out how you rank. Ask your boss outright, "If there were an opening, would Fred be more likely to get it than I?" When I was at Peat Marwick, one of my peer-group associates managed to learn that he was making about 5 percent less than two others of us. He concluded that he was not going to progress as rapidly as we were, and he was absolutely correct. When I differentiate between people in compensation in my own firm, it is because there is a difference. Knowing where you stand will enable you to plan intelligently for the future—either to develop ways to move up in rank, or to start figuring out where else to go.

Lower-ranking peers—and they generally do know who

they are—are likely to resent the success in their midst. But not always. If there is a true shining star among them, people often develop a strange combination of admiration and hate. They recognize the star's good performance and may even develop a proprietary feeling toward him or her and root for his or her success.

If you are outperforming your peers, make sure your peers know what you are doing, just as you inform your boss and your boss's boss. For your peers can help you. The rivalry they feel toward you will become obvious. The (perhaps grudging) admiration they express for your accomplishments will help direct attention to you. Even if they hate you, pure and simple, *that* can help. One of the best things that can happen to you, in fact, is to have your peer group sniping at you. If people troop into my office and complain over and over again about Sally, it's going to make me take a look at Sally, whom I may never have looked at before. If she is an irritant, *why* is she an irritant? Maybe she is doing something that everybody else should be doing but isn't.

If there is a star among your peers, and it is not you, carefully consider whether there is going to be room in the organization for both of you. If you can't beat him, you may elect to join him. Make a point of working well with him. As he goes forward, he can bring you up behind.

In the prime breakout years of thirty to thirty-five, relations among peers may grow especially tense. Yet the corporate culture dictates that even in the most intensely competitive situations there be a facade of cordiality. (There are pragmatic reasons for this, too. You may want your peers on your side in some future battle. You may want good references from them if you leave the company.) Very few companies encourage employees to eat their rivals. So don't. Cloak your ambition in the social graces as you carefully develop your strategy for breaking out.

PART 7

THE CORPORATE WOMAN

WHAT IF you're a woman?

Twenty years ago, this question would hardly have arisen. Women were as rare in executive positions as penguins at Disneyland. Of course, there were plenty of women working in corporations—as secretaries and clerks. "In those days my secretary was a terrific woman named Betty Martin," Lee Iacocca wrote in his autobiography. "If it weren't for the chauvinism built into the system, Betty would have been a vice-president—she was better than most of the guys who worked for me."

Many young women entering business today take for granted opportunities that had to be struggled for only a few years ago. When Rita Hauser, today one of the nation's leading attorneys and a partner in the firm of Stroock & Stroock & Lavan, went looking for her first job in international law in 1959, she set out with impressive credentials. She had a top American law degree and a French law degree. She spoke three European languages and had spent a significant amount of time abroad. "I went interviewing at the big firms," Hauser recalls, "and a lot of them simply were not hiring women." Frustrated, she took a job in the Justice Department. "I recently went up to Harvard Law School," she says, "and gave a talk on international law. Some two hundred and fifty kids showed up, and at least half, maybe more, were women. Many of them were interested in entering the field. And these young women didn't have a clue as to what it was like when you were knocking on the door, and they were saying to you, 'Terrific. You're wonderful. But we're just not hiring women.'"

Today, the big law firms, and the big corporations, *are* hiring women. Significant numbers of women go to work every year in most major industries. The first wave of entry-level women, hired five or ten years ago, have now reached the ranks of middle management. We have, in fact, just passed through a watershed era for women, as female middle managers have become common and widely accepted. They are now heading higher, into upper-middle-management jobs.

There are still very few women at the top, however. Our survey of more than 1,300 senior executives found that 98 percent were male. But there was a significant difference in the sex ratio from one age group to another. Only 1 percent of senior executives over fifty were female. Three percent of those in their forties were female. And 9 percent of those under forty were female. Clearly, as today's young executives move up the corporate ladder, the women among them will move up with their male peers.

This will, naturally, take time. Our surveyed executives have worked for their current employers for an average of seventeen years. Very few women have even been in the executive work force for seventeen years. A decade from now, the picture will be different. I expect women to fill 20 to 25 percent of senior positions by then. It is unrealistic to expect any faster movement. You have to spend fifteen years or so in middle management establishing your career before moving to the top, and most corporate women are still in the process of putting in those years. They are still paying their dues.

Moving from middle to senior management does not come easily for anyone—and it will be no snap for women. They will have to compete with highly motivated men for every available position, and their sex will give them no advantage. Companies that actively and vocally recruited bright young women for entry-level jobs a few years ago, and then encouraged the promotion of women to middle-management positions, do not feel the same obligation to move those women up from middle-management ranks. Any breaks women may have received when companies were eager to hire their first females are no longer operative. That party is over.

And the old party—the all-male party—has never completely ended. Old attitudes and old barriers survive, and they will make the climb to the top of the corporate ladder a tough one for women.

WOMEN VS. CORPORATE AMERICA

In 1982, Korn/Ferry International, in cooperation with the UCLA Graduate School of Management, surveyed three hundred women executives at major corporations. Their responses provide an interesting contrast to the results of our current (overwhelmingly male) survey:

Table 7–1

SEX AND THE SENIOR-EXECUTIVE PROFILE

Highlights from the Korn/Ferry Survey of Corporate Leaders (an overwhelmingly male group) in the Eighties, contrasted with results of the earlier Korn/Ferry Survey of 300 executive women.

	MEN	WOMEN
Average Age	51	46
Average Salary (1987 dollars)	$235,000	$115,500
Greatest Factor in Success	hard work	ambition, drive
Average Hours per Workweek	56	53
Days Spent Away on Business	49/yr.	33/yr.
Number of Vacation Days	14	16
Considered Fastest Route to the Top	marketing	marketing
Percentage Married	94%	41%

The women's survey included an item that asked respondents to identify "the greatest obstacle you had to

overcome to achieve your success." The greatest number
—39 percent—replied that it was "being a woman." No
other answer even came close. (In second place, with 11
percent, was "lack of confidence.") In response to another
question, 63 percent disagreed with the statement that
"barriers to women have fallen at the senior management
level."

Admittedly, this survey was taken several years ago,
and the women we polled were relative pioneers in the
corporate world (their average age in 1982 was forty-six).
But the problems they encountered have not disappeared.

"Women are still at a disadvantage," says Jane Evans, a
general partner in Montgomery Securities who has had a
well-chronicled and successful career at General Mills,
American Can, Monet Jewelers and elsewhere. "The reason that we're not making it to the very top is that men
don't feel comfortable with us. We're different than they
are. We're different from anything they've experienced in
their work environments. The male CEOs of most U.S.
corporations have never worked for a woman; they've
never worked with a woman; most of them have never
had a competent woman working for them; so they have
no knowledge of what a competent female executive is
like."

This is, of course, a chicken-and-egg problem. Men are
more likely to accept women in high-level management
jobs once they have seen women performing in high-level
management jobs. "It is rare to see women hospital ad-
ministrators," says Jane Hurd, who recently held the position of executive director and chief executive officer of
the prestigious Children's Hospital of Los Angeles.
"There are lots of women in mid-level hospital administration jobs, but it is a big jump from number two to
number one. The appointing authorities—the boards of
directors—are giving that top person a lot of bottom-line
responsibility, and it has taken time for women to prove
that they can handle that.... It takes a big buildup of the
perception of the whole group to make breakthroughs
start to happen."

There are institutional barriers to such breakthroughs as well. Much high-level business in America is conducted outside the office, on golf courses, at black-tie affairs, at luncheons and dinners. Women are not yet a part of the working social fabric of corporate life—the country clubs, the golf clubs, the social gatherings, the private luncheons. And social attitudes sometimes reduce their effectiveness even in public settings. Rita Hauser had difficulty for years arranging breakfast meetings with her law clients. The clients (mostly male) were afraid that bystanders would assume the breakfast was the culmination of an all-night rendezvous.

The closed doors women face in the corporate world have already spurred many of them to leave it. A higher percentage of women than men quit corporate jobs every year, many to go off on their own as entrepreneurs. With guts and imagination, these women are making their own rules and playing the game their own way. Women now own 25 percent of the nation's small businesses, up from a mere 5 percent in 1976.

For those who stick it out in the corporate world, the situation is far from hopeless. Women today represent some of the brightest, most aggressive, and most dedicated young executives in America. Time is on their side. While it is working its changes, women can help themselves by confronting the barriers that face them and adopting deliberate strategies to overcome them.

CAREER PATHS FOR WOMEN

When Jane Hurd graduated from the University of Arkansas in 1966, she became a schoolteacher, at $4,200 a year. She was a good teacher, but, she says, "It did not have the competitive aspects to it that I was really looking for. I wanted to be in charge. I have a competitive nature." Hurd moved to Los Angeles and began looking around for a career. When she asked a male acquaintance for advice, he replied, "Well, you could be a nurse, or a secretary, or a teacher." That's the way it was in 1968.

Hurd looked to a different, and seemingly unlikely, area for a challenging career. She took a civil service test, passed, and went to work as an administrative assistant at a Los Angeles County hospital. "It was an entry-level administrative job," she recalls: "inventory control, time-keeping systems, supervising the office staff. But I really loved it. This is what I was looking for—systems work and designing administrative methods." She rose rapidly until she was the highest-ranking administrative assistant in the system—executive assistant to the director of the Los Angeles County Department of Health Services.

Hurd's boss valued her highly in that job, but he unself-ishly gave her some excellent advice. "You only want to do this for about eighteen months," he said, "because this is not where the real action is. The real action is in line operations."

Hurd thus set off on the classic route to the top, by moving from a staff job to a line job. Her boss lent her to a large county hospital to gain some experience, and she soon landed the job of associate administrator at another hospital in the system. Two years later, she became chief administrator of yet another county hospital. Two years after that, at the age of thirty-four, she was recruited (by Korn/Ferry International) to become chief executive officer and executive director of Children's Hospital, a complex $100-million-a-year operation with 2,700 employees.

Hurd's career path was not unusual for women who came of age in the 1960s or before. Thirty-four percent of the female senior executives we surveyed began their careers in clerical or secretarial positions; that's the same number as those who began in managerial positions.

Today, women can approach management careers more directly. The fastest route to the top for women, our survey respondents said, is now marketing/sales. Finance/accounting is second. Ten years from now, the women predicted, general management will be the fastest track for women. The results were almost identical with those in our overwhelmingly male general management survey:

Table 7–2

FASTEST ROUTES TO THE TOP

	TODAY		10 YEARS FROM NOW	
	FOR WOMEN	FOR EVERYBODY	FOR WOMEN	FOR EVERYBODY
Marketing/Sales	30%	34%	24%	27%
Finance/Accounting	22	25	19	21
Professional/Technical	19	7	18	13
General Management	11	24	25	23
Consumer Affairs	6	—	2	—
Legal	4	—	2	—
Personnel	4	1	1	1
Production/Manufacturing	0	5	2	5
International	1	1	2	4

WOMAN-FRIENDLY COMPANIES

All companies are constrained by the same equal-opportunity laws to be fair to women, and all companies are influenced by the same social movements, but (to borrow a phrase from George Orwell), some companies treat women more equally than others.

When Jane Evans began her career in 1965, she got lucky. Upon finishing college, she took a job with Genesco, Inc., an apparel conglomerate, because it had an international division and she was interested in foreign affairs. She was unaware that as a woman, she could not have picked a better place to work.

"Genesco at that time was headed by Maxey Jarman," Evans now recalls, "who is a legend as far as putting women into positions of power. He really liked women, and he believed that in a business selling to women, women should be in positions to make decisions. So he created an environment where it was expected that capable women would succeed, and I give that culture an awful lot of credit for my own success." Five years after starting at Genesco, Evans was president of its I. Miller subsidiary.

Evans says she landed at Genesco "by accident, and it was one of the most fortunate accidents of my life." Young women today should not leave so much to chance. "There are clues in any company as to how good the culture is for a woman," Evans advises. "Unless a woman is willing to be the first pioneer to go crashing through barriers, and to get stomped on a lot, I don't think she should go to a company where there are no other women, where there is such a male culture that it probably isn't going to accept women for the next ten or twenty years. I encourage women to look at the boards of directors, and at annual reports. Look for those women who really do have responsible jobs in American business as opposed to those who are strictly tokens, like the people who serve on foundations or strictly philanthropic women. Look at the list of officers of a company. Are there any female names besides the assistant secretary? If not, steer away. You can also find out a lot about a company by talking to people who work for it." (You should also look to see if women are employed in upper middle-management jobs in corporate divisions as well as headquarters.)

And Evans has one more suggestion:

"Find out if the CEO has any daughters in their twenties or thirties who are in the work force. If so, he may be more interested in the culture for women in his own organization, because his daughters are coming up against discrimination for the first time in their lives. It's amazing how much those men have their eyes opened through their daughters. They say, 'How could they discriminate against *her*? She's just like *me*.'"

I raised this theory with one of the chief executives we interviewed for this book, a man who has four daughters working in marketing. "I think it's made me more positive toward women in business than maybe I would have been," he confirmed. "I was a classic male chauvinist at one time."

WOMAN-FRIENDLY INDUSTRIES

Perhaps even greater than the variations in the reception afforded women from company to company is the variation in attitudes toward women from industry to industry. Much of this is obvious to the unaided eye. Women partners in law firms are not unusual today. Nor are senior women executives in packaged-goods companies, advertising agencies, or entertainment or retailing firms. But you don't see many women near the top in steel, autos, chemicals, tires, or other heavy manufacturing industries. An extensive survey presented by Charlotte Decker Sutton and Kris K. Moore in the *Harvard Business Review* documented executives' perceptions of attitudes toward women in various industries. Most women surveyed said that women were at a severe disadvantage in manufacturing, construction, mining, oil, defense, aerospace, transportation, and public-utility companies. By a smaller percentage, men concurred (see Table 7–3).

Bright and dedicated women who sincerely want to enter one of those areas should not necessarily be deterred, however. "There's no question that there are some industries that have been less open to women," says Caroline Nahas, one of my partners at Korn/Ferry, who has substantial client and profit-center responsibilities there. "But as a result of that, many women have not pursued

Table 7–3

VARIATIONS IN PERCEPTIONS OF OPPORTUNITIES FOR WOMEN IN MANAGEMENT BY TYPE OF INDUSTRY

TYPE OF INDUSTRY	5 = Distinct advantage	4 = Equal advantage	3 = Moderate advantage	2 = Very little advantage	1 = Virtually no advantage	5 = Distinct advantage	4 = Equal advantage	3 = Moderate advantage	2 = Very little advantage	1 = Virtually no advantage
	AS SEEN BY MEN					AS SEEN BY WOMEN				
	5	4	3	2	1	5	4	3	2	1
Retail trade	31%	58%	10%	1%	0%	23%	49%	25%	2%	0%
Financial institutions	12	52	33	3	0	6	31	52	10	1
Manufacturing—consumer goods	1	36	46	15	1	0	17	53	26	3
Manufacturing—industrial goods	1	17	44	36	2	0	4	42	44	10
Advertising, media, publishing	24	64	10	1	0	10	57	32	2	0
Construction, mining, oil	0	9	24	54	14	0	1	16	50	33
Defense, space	4	32	40	21	4	1	7	29	48	15
Service trades	9	51	30	9	2	9	38	38	13	2
Transportation	3	28	48	21	1	0	11	40	41	8
Public utility	6	39	38	15	2	0	17	44	32	7

training that would prepare them for those industries. My philosophy is that you should pursue what's *you* and should not base your actions on what other people think you should do, or what looks as if it might be more available to you."

Nahas has actually lived that philosophy. After graduating from UCLA in 1970, she became a college recruiter for Bank of America, the first woman ever to have that job there. After only two years, she was promoted to head the bank's management-recruiting operation for southern California. "I just basically worked myself into the job," she says. "I had a tremendous amount of zeal.... There had never been a woman in that job. I was the first woman and the first *young* woman. It was very difficult for people to visualize me in that kind of role, making those kinds of decisions, and working with those key executives. But once they see you in the role, and they see you perform, those myths are dispelled. And that's the only way you can dispel them."

When Nahas moved on to another job, she was succeeded by a woman. And *that* woman was succeeded by a woman. The barrier was broken. Such barriers, Nahas argues, can and will be broken everywhere:

"If you're a woman thinking, 'I want to be in mining. I've always wanted to be in mining. My father was in mining, and this is something I love,' then I say, 'Go for it.' Don't say to yourself, 'Gee, I'll never make it.' Say, 'Look, since there haven't been any [women in mining], maybe I'll be the one who will be able to make the breakthrough, because *somebody* will get into those industries.'

"Going into a new field for women could even work to your advantage. While I feel I had all the qualities I think were needed to be successful in executive search, I've always felt the female quotient was an advantage for me, not a disadvantage. I'm not going to tell you that there weren't times when I was discouraged, when I felt that some people didn't give me a chance, but there were other people who, once they saw me perform, really went to bat for me, because they knew I was performing under difficult circumstances.

"Enough doors have been opened now that women will hopefully choose careers on the basis of what they really want to do, as opposed to what has been perceived before as the natural or obvious place to go.... But practicality's got to be a part of it. You have to evaluate yourself. Are you going to MIT? Are you going to be one of the best in your class? Do you have what it takes to compete?"

FEMALE GHETTOS

If you want to be a sales manager or a chief financial officer or an engineer, that's great. But be a little bit wary of committing yourself to personnel (or "human resources") or public relations. In many companies, these have become (in the years since Nahas and others blazed the trail) "women's jobs." The Sutton-Moore survey shows how these two areas (along with office management) are perceived as far more hospitable to women than other fields.

If you are interested in an area with a heavy proportion of women employees, then by all means pursue it. Do what you want to do. But be aware that entering such a field may typecast you and limit your future opportunities.

When Rita Hauser went looking for an international-law job in 1959, with her American and French law degrees, her language proficiency, and her foreign experience, she didn't stand a chance. She was looking outside the law profession's "women's ghetto."

"I had the problem of being a woman and picking an area of law in which there were virtually no women. There were preconceived notions: How could you be an

Table 7–4

VARIATIONS IN PERCEPTIONS OF OPPORTUNITIES FOR WOMEN IN MANAGEMENT BY FUNCTION

5 = Distinct advantage 4 = Equal advantage 3 = Moderate advantage 2 = Very little advantage 1 = Virtually no advantage

FUNCTION	AS SEEN BY MEN					AS SEEN BY WOMEN				
	5	4	3	2	1	5	4	3	2	1
Accounting	11%	75%	11%	2%	0%	6%	53%	38%	4%	0%
Engineering, R&D	9	41	38	12	1	2	13	49	31	6
Finance	8	58	29	5	0	3	34	51	11	1
Research	10	64	25	2	0	4	42	44	10	1
Labor relations	3	26	40	28	4	1	10	37	40	12
Marketing	11	62	26	2	0	7	41	43	9	0
Office management	24	64	12	1	0	24	52	22	2	0
Personnel	25	67	9	0	0	22	58	17	2	0
Production	1	20	44	31	3	0	11	38	41	9
Public relations	23	66	11	1	0	13	54	29	4	0

international lawyer? A woman? How were you going to travel, go abroad, all those things women didn't do then?

"At one or two of the firms, where I knew the senior people, they were nice enough to take me to lunch. They would say, 'Well, your record is so good, but you know, you'd have to go into estates and trusts.' Estates and trusts was where all the women were put. Something in me rebelled against that. I remember one very vivid discussion with a senior partner at one firm. When he told me they would take me into estates and trusts, I said, 'Absolutely not. I am not going to do that. I am going to find my way, no matter how, to do what I'm interested in and what I'm trained for.'"

Through talent and extraordinary willpower, Hauser ultimately succeeded in having the career she wanted. If she had gone into the women's ghetto of estates and trusts, she might well still be there today.

Years later, Mary Cunningham came out of Harvard Business School and went to work as an executive assistant to William Agee at Bendix. She was enough of a careerist to scrupulously avoid what she described in her memoir as "merely women's stuff." "I kept trying to move away from the direction of personnel and PR," she wrote. "Personnel and public relations are the most common areas in which women are made corporate vice presidents and therefore don't have much prestige among most men."

Today, this judgment may be a little harsh. Just as women managed years ago to break *into* the areas which then became women's ghettos, so are they now beginning to break *out of* them. One woman we interviewed, a vice president of one of the nation's ten largest advertising agencies, works in her agency's media department, which is an advertising version of a female ghetto. "When I first started, ten years ago, there was still a stigma attached to being in the media department," she says. "There are a lot of women who have been media buyers for twenty or twenty-five years. They started as assistant buyers. They became buyers. That is all they were ever going to be, and that's what they still are."

This woman does not, however, foresee the same fate for herself. She is already a department supervisor and a vice president. "I resolved that I wasn't going to be one of those women who was a buyer for twenty-five years. And I don't have to be. The media area is no longer a dead end. In the old days, women could not become associate media directors or media directors. Those were always men, who came from the planning side of the media department, as opposed to the buying side. By the time I'd been in the business five years, everything had changed. There are a lot of avenues open to me that weren't open to women when I started out. I have already made inroads in what women can do in my department, and I think I can go much higher in the advertising world."

The moral: nowadays starting out in a "women's area" may not doom you to spend the rest of your career there. But do take a look around (look especially at what has happened to your predecessors in those areas) before you jump in.

ADAPTING TO THE MALE CULTURE

"I like to equate it to a foreign assignment," Jane Evans says of being a woman in the corporate world. "You need to know that you're speaking a foreign language in a foreign country."

Evans suggests that women be careful about both *how* they talk and what they talk *about.* "There are some stereotypes that women should not reinforce in their conversations with men. Unless they know the men well, I don't think they should talk about whatever problems they're having raising children."

What they *should* talk about is business.

"It's amazing to me the number of young women who

don't read *Fortune* and *The Wall Street Journal*. Or else they don't seem to pick up the information, or they haven't learned how to use the information as an ice-breaker. It's great, if you're standing next to someone at a cocktail party or whatever, if you can say, 'Did you see that article on Boone Pickens this morning?' That can get the conversation rolling on a level that men are going to feel comfortable about."

Even in a strict business context, Evans warns, women may stand out by the language they use. "Women tend to be more enthusiastic than men and to show their emotions more around a business discussion. I think we have to temper that. When I'm with a lot of women I'll be much more expressive than when I've got a bunch of men around. Because most of the products that I've dealt with all my life are things a woman can wear, we might try them on, and we'll 'ooh' and 'ahh.' We can make men so uncomfortable doing that." With men around, Evans restrains herself.

Any woman, asked by her boss for her opinion of a new advertising campaign, would be well advised not to reply that she thinks it is "darling."

"Words like that make men feel uncomfortable," Evans says. She places a great deal of emphasis on what does or does not make men uncomfortable, because she recognizes that women, for the foreseeable future, must rely on male bosses and male colleagues for their advancement. "Somehow it is incumbent upon us as women to make men as comfortable in our presence as possible, because we are still the ones that are at a disadvantage.... Even though I serve on the boards of two major U.S. corporations [Equitable Life and Philip Morris], a lot of the men on the boards treat me like we're on a date, in spite of the fact that we're dealing with issues like corporate finance. It's unbelievable. They say, 'Oh, you look wonderful,' and the kinds of things they would never say to another man.... They have a lot of difficulty fighting with me, or even getting into a dialogue where there's any sort of conflict or contention. These are the superficial relationships. I'm not talking about the men I deal with on a daily basis, the men who report to me, or the men whom I report to.... It's that initial comfort level that takes quite a while to get through.

"I use humor with great regularity. I think it's one of the most important attributes I have. It's not scathing. One of my favorite lines that I use in my speeches is that because most men have never worked for one of us divine creatures, I sometimes feel like I'm a one-woman campaign of letting men know that we're safe to deal with. And I'm fond of quoting the Mae West line 'So many men, so little time.' "

(In her memoir, Mary Cunningham acknowledged that her dead-serious personal style may have made things tougher for her in the hostile atmosphere she encountered at Bendix: "I'd walk into a meeting, notebook and pencil in hand, and in my very businesslike manner, start talking about market shares and P/E ratios. This didn't win me points. In retrospect I might have been better off had I tried to crack a few jokes.")

Evans has often been mentioned as a likely candidate to be one of the first women CEOs of a Fortune 500 corporation (after Katharine Graham of The Washington Post Company, Linda Wachner of Warnaco, and Elizabeth Claiborne Ortenberg of Liz Claiborne).

"I don't know if I will be," Evans says. "It's going to take a board of directors of men to put me there, and I don't know if it's possible to make that many men comfortable."

"PINKS" AND "BLUES"

A prerequisite for making the people around you comfortable is being comfortable with yourself. "Do not apologize for being a woman," says Jane Hurd, who has risen to the top in a male-dominated field. "There are things about being a woman that make you a better manager, such as being sensitive to other people. Little girls are trained since they could toddle around to be sensitive to other people's wants and needs. Little boys are not taught that. Little boys are taught to be independent, self-centered, exploring, and analytical. Little girls are taught to be cute and sensitive to other people.... This automatically puts us in a management style that I think is very effective, which is team building, consensus development, making people feel a part of the group. If you look at *In Search of Excellence*, if you look at the characteristics of successful companies, you'll see they are people-oriented. They know what the customer wants. They practice 'management by walking around.' They listen to their employees."

Hurd gives a popular speech that she calls "Pinks and Blues." She identifies "pink" personality characteristics as those that are traditionally female—being intuitive, imaginative, creative, sensitive—and "blue" characteristics as those that are traditionally male—being analytical, ambitious, thoughtful, decisive.

"There is a lot of confusion in women about their 'pink' aspects," Hurd says. "Women wonder, 'Are they good? Are they bad? Should I play them down and pretend that they don't exist while I build up my "blue" aspects?'

"We all—men and women—have both pink and blue characteristics. And we need to have both to be successful managers. So women should not play down their pinks in favor of their blues, because they would be giving up half of their personality that can be very beneficial in a lot of management situations.

"On the other hand, women have to have the blues or they will not be successful. And people will assume that they do not have the blues. When a hiring authority looks at a woman, the question in his mind is 'Can she be tough enough? Could she fire somebody if she had to?' So while women have to nurture their pink aspects, they also have to demonstrate their blue aspects to the people they want to hire or promote them.

"If I go into a job interview to be assistant administrator of a hospital, the administrator is going to assume my pink characteristics. He is going to assume that I will always be sensitive to the doctors' needs. And that I am never going to get him in trouble by being overbearing. That I am going to be able to make nursing work well with the physicians, and so on. He will assume all of that, as pluses.

"But he will also have a question in his mind about my blues. 'Can she make a profit? Can she lay off people if she needs to? Can she be tough enough?'

"A woman has to demonstrate she has these capabilities by saying, 'Here is how I handled things in my previous job. There was a situation where I had a department head who was not performing. I counseled him, and he was still not performing. So I had to let him go.' Or, 'When I took over the department we were losing three hundred thousand dollars a year. And this year we made a six-hundred-thousand-dollar profit.' These are the things a woman has to bring up. A woman doesn't need to bring up how sensitive she is.

"And this works the other way too. If you are a man coming in and interviewing with me, I am going to assume that you are going to be able to do the tough stuff. But I am going to wonder, 'Is he going to alienate all the doctors? Is he going to run roughshod over nursing?' So you need to tell me, 'Here is how I handled a very delicate person problem.'"

FAMILY ISSUES

One constant factor in the lives of successful executives is that their careers have been of paramount importance to them. In every case, their careers have been at least as important as their personal family lives. Sometimes, they have been more so. Seventy-three percent of the executives in our survey said that *if* they had more free time, they would spend it with their spouses. Executive after executive spoke in our interviews of how "understanding" their wives were, how they raised the kids and took care of the house and did not complain that their husbands weren't around very much or that at inconvenient times, they had to pack up the house and the kids and move to distant cities to suit their husbands' careers.

The advent of women in the corporate work force has upset the applecart of career–family relations. To accommodate the built-in conflicts there, many members of the first generation of women in business made the terrible sacrifice of dispensing with family life altogether. Our 1982 survey of women executives found that 48 percent were divorced, separated, or never married (compared with only 5 percent of the men in our current survey). Sixty-one percent of the women had no children (compared with 5 percent of the men).

Most younger women working for corporations today are, or will be, attempting to combine their careers with family life. They are, or will be, running head-on into several difficult problems.

THE TWO-CAREER FAMILY

In the traditional corporate family, the wife receives no paycheck, but she plays a role in company life nonetheless. She takes part in the social life that is an essential element in boosting her husband's career, entertaining at home and attending outside events on her husband's arm. If her husband is a top executive, she has to look on with adoring attention while he makes speeches she may have heard a dozen times before. She has to be part of the loyal company "team," or hubby may be in trouble. There are companies that still take a careful look at an executive's wife as part of evaluating *his* suitability for promotion. A strong argument has been made that such corporate wives are in fact performing a job—and ought to be paid for it.

The female advertising-agency vice president we interviewed recalls her own mother's unwilling-but-effective performance as a corporate spouse. "I remember years and years of listening to her complain that she and my father had to go out and entertain clients. If they were having his clients over for dinner, she would be bitching all afternoon: 'Why am I cooking this dinner for people I can't stand?' And then the doorbell would ring and she'd put a big smile on her face and say, 'I haven't seen you in so long. I'm so happy you could come.'"

This woman's mother may not have always liked it, but she did the job. Like most corporate spouses of her generation, she had no job outside the home. Today's career women simply don't have time for hostessing. It is just about impossible to be a loyal and enthusiastic corporate wife if you are engrossed in your own corporate career. Your schedule is full; your loyalties are divided; you may, in fact, be in need of a corporate "wife" of your own.

Today, the advertising executive finds her parents' roles reversed in her own marriage. "My husband sometimes has to play the corporate spouse," she says. "My boss, who is a woman, is in our New York office. She comes here two or three times a year, usually with her husband, and we have to spend the evenings with them. She and I talk business, and Ron [my husband] has to make small talk with her husband.

"We also socialize with executives from the local television stations. They are all male, and they bring their wives. If the conversation turns to business, Ron ends up talking to the wife. Usually, they start out by talking about how funny it is that she is talking to him. Then it usually evolves into talking about Ron's business. Fortunately, he is an athletic-clothing retailer, so he and the women can always talk about leotards or jogging shoes. . . .

"Ron goes to work in his stores in tennis shoes and an

Izod shirt. To go out in the evening with me, we had to buy him some sport coats and ties. He hates them. When he first began to socialize with my business associates, he found it interesting. Now there are certain people he likes and is happy to see. But he definitely balks on other occasions. I tell him he has to do it. Sometimes I hold up one of my paycheck stubs and I say, 'See this? Do you want to see another one of these? Put your tie on.' "

Even if a two-career couple manage to do enough happy socializing to keep two companies content (the advertising executive sometimes entertains sales reps her husband does business with, and she doesn't always like it), a troublesome day of reckoning will await on the horizon. One day, inevitably, one party to the marriage will be asked to make an essential career move to another city at a time when such a move would be a severe disadvantage to the other's career. This situation has already resulted in commuter marriages—he's a vice president in Boston; she's a sales manager in Seattle; they have brunch in Chicago twice a month. In most cases, however, a decision must be made. Whose career is more important? (It is quite possible today, among people in their thirties, for it to be the wife who is earning the big bucks and has the greater potential.) Who is willing to sacrifice? What is really important to her? To him?

These questions ought to be considered before they arise, for the sake of both one's marriage and one's career.

THE CORPORATE MOTHER

The most difficult questions career women face have to do with children—when to have them, how to care for them, how to reconcile their demands with the demands of employment.

Many women are ducking these questions, at least temporarily, by putting off starting families. Throughout the corporate world, one encounters married women in their early thirties who've intended to have children but just haven't gotten around to it yet. A not-atypical young woman engineer told *Fortune* a few years ago that she and her husband weren't planning on having kids until "my career is well established [and] we have all the material things we want.... With our lifestyle, we can't afford good child care now and all the things we like ... skiing in the mountains, entertaining around the pool at home, houseboating on Lake Powell in Utah, and weekend waterskiing on the Baja peninsula in Mexico."

Some of these women will never find the "right" time to have a child. But many others will decide, as the biological clock ticks on, that they are going to have a kid or two and make the best of it. Fortunately for them, corporations are just beginning to accommodate executive mothers.

Nevertheless, the first quandary they will face has to do with maternity leave. When Jane Evans was pregnant in 1974, she was vice president of international marketing for Genesco. She was spending half her time outside the country, and continued to do so through most of her pregnancy. "Fortunately, I wasn't very large," she says. "So I traveled through my eighth month, even though Alitalia almost threw me off one of their planes. They were afraid I might give birth right there on board."

Evans returned to work ten days after her son was born. "I was at a very high level," she says. "It would have been absolutely unfair to the business, to myself, and to people who worked with and for me to take any more time off than I had to."

Evans advises young women: "If you're really serious about your career, don't expect to take a long maternity leave. If you can get back soon, you really send a signal to the organization that you're serious about your career."

Despite such attitudes, most companies make provisions for six to eight weeks of paid maternity leave and unpaid leaves of three to six months. The advertising vice president we interviewed recently had her first child at the age of thirty-one and managed to take a ten-week leave (by adding sick days and accumulated vacation time to the six weeks her company provided). She was extremely careful, however, to see that her leave would not hurt her career. She accomplished that primarily by continuing to work the whole time she was away.

"I went on a big campaign," she says, "to prove that I wasn't going to be the type of person who went off to have a baby and stopped being responsible. A lot of people go on maternity leave and just say, 'Bye. See you in a few months.' I felt I just couldn't disappear for that long for any reason. So I was in constant contact with my office. I had the woman who works under me come to my house every week with my mail, and we went over all the problems. I talked to her three or four times a week. I went into the office once a week. I talked to my boss in New York at least once a week. I talked to *her* boss twice while I was home.

"I was hired to be responsible for running my office, and that's what my employers expect of me. And I felt that if I didn't prove to them that I could fit my family into my career, my raises and/or promotions over the next couple of years might not be forthcoming. I felt I had to prove to them that while I was gone I was still responsible; but I did sometimes resent it. Sometimes they would call me up when I had my baby crying on my shoulder and I had been up three or four times in the middle of the night and I was exhausted. And they were calling me and sending things over and I wanted to say, 'Just let me get my life organized here and let me alone.' That is nothing my husband will ever have to go through. That is nothing anybody's husband will ever have to go through."

From her employer's point of view, her maternity leave was exemplary. Women can be less conscientious and still not harm their careers. Even a six-month leave need have no negative impact, as long as everybody understands (including your husband) that you intend to return to work. Over the long scheme of a career, taking six months out to have a child is almost irrelevant.

Anything longer than six months, however, begins to be a problem (just as a man who asks for more than six months off to sail around the world might develop a sudden problem in *his* career).

A *series* of six-month leaves is also likely to present a problem. As a practical matter, most women who are in middle management today have probably delayed child-bearing so long that they are likely to have only one or two children, if any. Those who choose to have more will risk harm to their careers. Any valuable employee, male or female, who asks for six months off for any reason is likely to get it, although the employer might grouse about it. To take a second six-month leave and return to the same career path, the employee would have to be *really* valuable. A third six-month leave ... it's not easy.

Not surprisingly, Jane Evans has a single child. "Possibly, I might have had another child, if I hadn't had the schedule that I have and if I hadn't been at the level that I am, or was even then," she says. "One's enough for the kind of life that I lead."

And Evans, naturally, employed a full-time child-care worker from the moment her son was born. Hauser (who has two children) employed a "spectacularly good house-keeper," she says. "The children were extremely attached to her ... and there was a certain pang about that in the beginning, that they were more involved with her than they were with me. I accepted it. If it had not been for Virginia [the housekeeper], I could not have stayed abroad for long periods of time. When the kids are teenagers, that's when they throw all this up to you. You know: 'Where were you then?' And you just say to yourself, 'It'll work itself out.' "

Working women are indeed subject to pangs of doubt about their children. "I go back to work in three days," said the advertising executive (whom we interviewed just as her maternity leave was ending), "and I have mixed emotions about it. I have a ten-week-old baby, who is just beginning to do things, whom I care more about than any human being I have ever cared about, and I am going to leave her all day long in the care of a woman I met two weeks ago."

It is perhaps not fair that women executives, and not men, feel these worries. (The kids have two parents, after all.) But we are dealing here with social arrangements of great age and power, and it is women who are caught between old ways and new.

Becoming a top executive is every woman's right, and well within the grasp of many women's capabilities. But to succeed, a woman probably has to want success more than her male peers, to work harder, and to make more sacrifices.

PART 8

BLOCKED!

AT LEAST once a year, the rising executive has to take a long, hard look around and decide if he or she is facing any brick walls. Are there any impediments on the upward path?

Blocks do crop up in every career. The successful acknowledge them and deal with them. First of all, they try to see them coming. "When trouble is sensed well in advance it can easily be remedied," Machiavelli wrote. "As the doctors say of a wasting disease, to start with it is easy to cure but difficult to diagnose; after a time, unless it has been diagnosed and treated at the outset, it becomes easy to diagnose but difficult to cure."

The successful are never passive. They do not just sit at their desks day after day and assume everything will work out for the best. When they are stymied by a block, they take steps to surmount it. They do not "live with" a bad situation. They change it. If nothing is happening, good or bad, they shake things up. They do not sit and look at the scenery.

There is a wide variety of common career blocks, and a variety of effective responses to them:

BLOCKED BY ONE'S OWN LIMITATIONS

This is a self-imposed block. It results from a failure of initiative or imagination. Those who suffer from it are generally doing their jobs well, but they are not doing them extraordinarily well. They often fail to realize what their employers value most.

"What I tell new people," says William Smithburg, chairman of Quaker Oats, "is this: In your first year or two, if you're one of seven or eight people working on a brand, there will be a lot of numbers work. Do what your boss asks you to do. Do it well. But at the end of one year, ask yourself, 'What ideas do I now have for this brand? What ideas do I have for something different?'

"Say you've been on Cap'n Crunch for a year. You're an intelligent person. You've done everything you've been asked to do. You've produced the financial reports. You've been working for the sales force on all the logistics and trade allowances. Now, after one year, what can you suggest we do that is new and unique and different? Put it down in writing and give it to your brand manager. If he or she rejects it, don't worry. Try another idea in three months. Try another one in three more months. Keep coming up with ideas.

"A few years ago Cap'n Crunch ran a promotion in which children called an 800 number. The brand manager at that time didn't necessarily come up with that idea, but he dealt with the outside creative source, the promotions consultant, who did. He managed the process, and the brand just took off. Twenty-four million children called.

"That manager was on the brand for two years and was then promoted. His next three successors in a row came up with no such excellent promotions, and the brand slowly began to decline...I said, 'Why don't the brand managers take the same telephone promotion that we ran and change the names of the characters if they can't come up with anything new? There's a whole new group of kids under six years old by now who didn't see the original promotion.' But people do not like to do what the guy before them did.

"The fourth brand manager (after the one who ran the telephone promotion) came on two years ago. Normally, I don't have a lot of direct discussions with brand managers, but I happened to know this one. So I said, 'Let's try to do something exciting. Go out and talk to ad agencies. Go out and talk to promotional suppliers. Talk to the promotions consultant who came up with the telephone idea. Come up with an effective promotion!' The brand manager did that, and Cap'n Crunch had a big promotion (in which it was announced that Cap'n Crunch was lost and children participated in solving the mystery of his disappearance). When he brought it in to show it to me, I said, 'Fine...Now start worrying about next year.'

"The point is: think ahead, be innovative, take prudent risks. The money spent on the mystery promotion was enormous—$10 million or $15 million over 90 days. During the period, when the brand had just a mediocre premium or a mail-in promotion with 'me-too' commercials, it may have run $7 million or $8 million a quarter. To do the real big one costs more. There's a risk in that. But you have to do it."

And what happened to the managers who ran the "me-too" campaigns?

"Two are with other companies. Their failure was a failure to take risks. On the other hand, we have a guy running Gatorade now. Earlier in his career, he happened to introduce a cereal that failed. But that's not the end of the world, to have a failure. In fact, he has been promoted several times since then. I want people who are willing to take the risks. The biggest risk of all is to take no risks."

BLOCKED BY ONE'S OWN SUCCESS

This is a pleasant sort of block, until its consequences begin to come clear. Those who suffer from it are performing their jobs *too* well—or at least, well enough that their employers do not want to shift them out of their present positions. They are so important in their jobs that replacing them there would be a hardship.

One deals with this situation by keeping one's career goals in mind at all times. Identify the next position to which you wish to be promoted, make a point of satisfying whatever criteria that job requires, and make sure your employer knows you expect to get it once you deserve it. Finally, make things a little easier for your employer—groom your own successor for your present job.

A similar kind of block is faced by a talented young man I know who works for one of the Big Eight accounting firms. His employers are very pleased with him and have high hopes for him. They are, in fact, grooming him for a partnership. To develop his skills in managing an office and building up a practice, they have assigned him to run the firm's office in a minor city. They do not intend to keep him out of the mainstream forever, just long enough to polish some of the skills they seek in their partners. He will be away long enough, however, to miss many other opportunities. In his previous assignment, he was handling the accounts of major corporate clients, any one of whom might have been sufficiently impressed with him to offer him a job and turn his career in a different direction. Now, in addition to being out of sight and out of mind, he is working in areas that will be of no use to any employer but his present one. He is becoming a good "organization man" for one organization; he is no longer gaining the kind of experience that will make him valuable to others. He is at a career crossroads, and he has got to recognize that. If he is certain that his goal is to be a partner in the accounting firm, then he is on the right track. If he aspires to anything else in the world of business, he must make a move soon.

BLOCKED BY BEING IN THE WRONG PLACE

There are certain kinds of companies and certain divisions within companies that an ambitious executive should beware of. Family-owned companies, for example, may offer limited opportunities for promotion because the top spots are filled by family members. If the top spots are *not* filled by family members, there is still rea-

Table 8–1

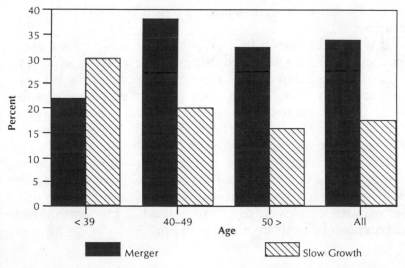

PRINCIPAL THREAT TO CAREER

son for caution. The family may be inclined to sell the company out.

The most common "wrong-place" blockage occurs in companies that are candidates for sale or merger, or are simply on the way down. Our surveyed senior executives listed slow growth and prospective mergers or reorganizations as the primary threats to their careers.

Companies that face possible sale or merger are not bad places for everyone, however. If you were making a career in the broadcasting division of NBC when RCA was acquired by General Electric, you had nothing special to fear. NBC was simply exchanging one parent corporation for another. But if you are on the general legal staff of a merging company, you may well be in trouble. Newly merged companies probably don't need two general legal staffs.

Declining companies are, in most cases, good places to leave. Jane Evans resigned from Genesco in 1974 when the company "had begun to experience some severe problems," she says. "I was really questioning what there was going to be for me, or for anybody else, at Genesco at that point, because they were selling off divisions, and they were really paring back the company, and they were having some very unsuccessful years." Just at that point, a headhunter called Evans on behalf of American Can. She took the new job—a prudent decision under the circumstances.

If you find yourself in a division with a shrinking market share, or in a troubled company or a dying industry, you ought to begin to look elsewhere. You will be best off beginning to do so before your present employer's problems have come to a head. Bad situations generally take a while to develop. Be alert for them. There is an art to knowing when to get off a dying horse.

But if you have nowhere special to go—no headhunters are knocking on your door—you may have to attempt something even more ambitious than leaving your problem-ridden employer: to try to solve the problem. Major careers can be built by not giving up.

"Back in 1969," recalls Norman Blake, "I was in Oklahoma City, working for the General Electric Comany's information-devices department, which was a manufacturer of computer equipment. At that time, G.E. was really kind of faltering in terms of its competitiveness within that industry. And there was a constant reorganization mode within the company, so there was a real sense of insecurity and volatility. They just kept changing the guard. As a result, a lot of the management were very insecure in their jobs and were very much in a risk-averse mode and were not very inclined to take bets in terms of new approaches and strategies. Everybody was protecting their vested interests and not moving forward.

"At that time, I was a sales specialist and, believe it or not, a systems-designer/product-planner type all kind of rolled into one. From my perspective, I saw no clear direction in the business. The organization was in a very chaotic state of affairs. There was no momentum in the organization whatsoever. I viewed myself as being in a situation which was not conducive to my own personal development and to gaining recognition for whatever I might achieve. My boss was a middle-aged fellow and very concerned about his own job security. He was a very nice person, but I recognized that he was not going to be the leader and take any sort of risk-taking posture. And they could have used some risk. Basically, nobody took a position on anything.

"Everybody was frustrated. We were just wallowing in mediocrity. [My peers] just went with the tide. They thought, 'Just wait. It will all get better.' I wasn't interested in waiting for someone else to make it better. I was interested in trying to make a contribution to the business and through that to have an opportunity to grow and develop myself.... So I undertook, of myself, to do a complete analysis of the business. I asked permission to be, on my own time, an internal consultant and assess where I thought the problems were, in terms of our competitive posture as a business vis-à-vis the marketplace, in terms of our technology base, in terms of the quality of our product line, as well as the organization, the quality of management, direction, and so on.

"I asked if it would be okay if I did it on my own. I asked my boss, and he really didn't say yes and he really didn't say no. I didn't want to push it, but I asked him to write a letter allowing me to interview the managers of the various businesses with the understanding that I would present him with my report, and he could decide what he wished to do. I wrote up the letter and had my boss sign it in a weak moment.

"So I spent about two months, on my own time, interviewing the senior managers, as well as some of the key technical and marketing people. I saw them at lunches or first thing in the morning or at night, so I wasn't conflicting with their schedules. Then I did some external research, obtaining market-research information, and so on. There was information available from consulting studies that the company itself had entered into. I got information from salesmen in the field, and product-description information that a salesman would give to a prospective client. I went through an exhaustive analysis and then presented a game plan to the section managers that ultimately got to a general manager of that department.... I drew ideas from throughout the organization and tried to put them into a framework by which the decision-makers could more readily discern what things could be done. One of the things that developed from that was the whole area of on-line systems.... It was very much a challenging position statement, and it received varying degrees of either wholehearted endorsement or wholehearted resentment on the part of some of the key figures in the business."

Blake's audacious consulting project was a success. It won him recognition, and the ideas in his report were a positive contribution to the company.

"After I presented the report, I was asked by the general manager to go back to some of the product section managers and discuss with them more specifically some of these program ideas. In one of these cases, I was asked to stay on. 'Would you like to work on this project?' I said yes. And from that, I got involved in new technology and the new-product-development area."

Blake's career began to move—because he had done something to help his employer's business move.

BLOCKED BY ONE'S BOSS

Your upward mobility within a corporation will be heavily dependent on who is in front of you. If your boss is within a few years of your age, you had better decide in a hurry if he or she is promotable. If the answer is no—he or she is a turkey—you had better start looking for a way to get out from under that boss, or to leapfrog him.

If your boss *is* promotable, the best thing you can do is help him get promoted as quickly as possible. Make sure you understand how he is evaluated by *his* boss. Then help him accomplish those things his superiors value the most. Visibility is always important; help your boss get it. When you do something great, share the limelight with him. You don't want to outshine your boss, and you don't want to get on his wrong side. You want to get him promoted, and you want him to recommend you to be his successor. With the right relationship with your boss, you can follow him all the way up to the top of the organization.

Then, of course, things get a little crowded. Companies have only a single CEO. It may be too soon for you to start worrying about that position yourself, but you never know. The day may come.

It didn't come soon enough for Harry Gray when he was at Litton Industries. Gray, who recently retired as chairman of United Technologies, worked at Litton from

1954 to 1971. By the late 1960s, he had the number-three
job there and was looking forward to moving up.

His way was blocked by CEO Charles "Tex" Thornton,
who had founded the company a few months before Gray
joined it. "In the early days," Gray recalls, "Tex used to
have a philosophy that he expressed to a number of us
that nobody should be the CEO of a growing company
after age fifty-five. Nobody told him he had to say that,
but he did." On many occasions over the years, Thornton
talked about his impending retirement; but he never retired. When Thornton was fifty-eight, Gray finally enter-
tained an offer from a headhunter to go to what was then
United Aircraft. "I had given him three years past his
own self-proclaimed retirement age," Gray says. Even
then, the two men had a final meeting on the subject.

"He was very upset about [my job offer from United]....
He talked to me all day, from nine o'clock in the morning
until just about supper. We had lunch together. He didn't
do anything else. And I kept asking him, 'What are you
going to do about your plan to retire?' And he kept not
answering the question. I made the inquiry a minimum of four times.... I said, 'Just give me a time frame.
I don't care if you're telling me it's going to be three to
five years. But I've got to have one.' The key point was
that he wouldn't."

Gray took the job at United. More than a decade later,
Thornton died—still CEO of Litton.

John Chamberlin ran into a similar block, and scrambled his way around it, a couple of times at Lenox, Inc.
Chamberlin was working at General Electric in 1970
when a recruiter called. "He said that the chairman of
Lenox, who was then about fifty-three or fifty-four, had
run the company for many years, had made himself a little money, and was interested in having a successor come
on board.... So I went to Lenox and the chairman, John
Tassie, gave me part of the company to run. He ran the
other parts. I was very happy there. However, it became
evident that Tassie, who was a brilliant marketer and a
classic entrepreneur, was not about to [retire]. He told me
when I first got there that he wanted to go down to the

beaches of Puerto Rico, but it was clear to me that that kind of guy is never going to go down to the beaches of Puerto Rico. He was going to work as long as he could."

After eighteen months at Lenox, Chamberlin was offered the job of general manager of General Electric's housewares division. "I decided to talk to them. I looked at Tassie and concluded again, 'He isn't going to give up. I'll be here for ten years doing the same thing.'" Chamberlin took the job at G.E.

"In 1976 I got a call from Tassie again. He had had a heart attack. He called me up and said he was definitely going to leave. I said, 'John, I'll believe that when I see it.' He said, 'I want to talk to you.' I said, 'Okay, fine, but I'm not going to come back because you'll never leave.' He said, 'I am.' I said, 'Okay, I'll come back, but I want a contractual agreement that you're going to leave. There's no way I'm coming back without that.'"

Chamberlin got the contract, went back to Lenox, and became CEO. But this kind of career block has more lives than a cat. In 1983, Lenox was bought out by the Brown-Forman Corporation. "Essentially," says Chamberlin, "I was again running a division." In 1985, he took a job as president and chief operating officer of Avon.

BLOCKED BY A LOUSY BOSS

Ideally, throughout your career, you will work for people you respect. It will be obvious to you why they are sitting where they are sitting and why you are sitting somewhere beneath them. It is easy to be motivated working for such people. They will move up the corporate hierarchy, and you will move up behind them.

Such bosses do exist; but so do the other kind—the

run-of-the-mill, insecure, screwed-up manager who will neither do his own job especially well nor level with you about how you are doing yours.

If your boss is incompetent, you have got to get out from under him, leapfrogging him if possible, just moving laterally if necessary.

If, for the moment, you are trapped behind a clunker of a boss, do not despair. Your boss's shortcomings may be obvious not only to you but also to his superiors. Find out. The corporate grapevine can help you here. So might the industry grapevine outside your own company. (When you want to hear what is wrong in your company, often the best way to do it is to talk to your competition.)

If word comes back, either way, that your boss is widely considered a jerk, then he may already be on his way out, which will solve your problem. If he is not going to be fired, you will at least know that there is sympathy for your predicament among the higher-ups. Your temporary lack of progress will not be held against you.

Such a situation was faced by Raymond Dempsey, chairman of the European American Bank, when he was a young assistant treasurer at Bankers Trust in the early 1960s. He was working in a group that was responsible for loans in five large industrial states. "It was, incredibly, probably the most profitable of all the units in the bank, but it was not legitimately adventuresome. It was run by a guy who was older and very conservative....It was probably the worst year I ever had in my life, working for this guy. I was allowed to go to places like Wapakoneta, Ohio. I was not allowed to go to any big cities. I was not allowed to call on customers. I was only allowed to call on prospects, people who *might* do business with the bank. I thought, 'I am not learning anything. I am not growing.'"

For his frustrations, Dempsey blamed his boss. "The guy was known as a disaster. But at banks in those days, no matter how bad a disaster you were, you worked for-ever. Nobody ever got fired."

Dempsey decided he had to take action on his own. "I

got to the point where I really felt that if you were legitimately not learning and if you were legitimately being held back, you had two choices. You tell the person who can do something about it, or you quit. What you should never do is do nothing.

"I complained to a guy who was my boss's boss's boss. I said, 'I don't want to work for this guy anymore. I am not learning anything.' And the guy had a choice. He could change [the situation], he could tell me to shut up, or he could fire me. But you never got fired, so...." Dempsey was moved laterally to work under someone he respected.

Lateral moves are also a prescription for another kind of boss blockage: your boss is perfectly competent but you and he just don't see eye to eye. You disagree about life in general—or, more to the point, you disagree about your talents and prospects in particular. Whenever you're in the running for a promotion, you want your boss to want you to get that promotion. If your boss thinks you're unpromotable, you've got a serious problem.

You should always know what your boss thinks about you, as I discussed earlier. If he doesn't think much of you, it may be because you have failed to understand his objectives and agenda and thus failed to produce what he needed. You should always know what your boss needs from you and do all that you can to deliver it.

If the problem is deeper than that—you could singlehandedly deliver a doubling of company revenues and your boss still wouldn't think much of you—then you have got to get out from under that boss. This kind of thing happens a great deal; the sooner you recognize it, the better off you are going to be.

While you are waiting to make your move, you are not necessarily dead. If you are doing good work, make sure your boss's boss knows about it. If he does—and the work really *is* good—your unenthusiastic boss cannot block you.

BLOCKED BY ONE'S PEERS

Some companies are management-rich. Most are not; most are screaming for truly good executives. But there are some companies with excellence in depth. If your company has a large corps of talented people of approximately the same age marching along at approximately the same pace, decide if you are willing to wait five years to see if you will be one of the few tapped to break away from the pack. Now might be the time to move somewhere where you will be more appreciated. That may be a smaller company or division, or a company or division that obviously needs talented help.

Regardlesss of how many peers you have, you may be blocked if your boss has a favorite fair-haired boy, and it is not you. If you are always going to rank behind the favorite, and there is room for only one, it is time to move elsewhere, probably laterally within your own company. If you are still on reasonably good terms with your boss, hit him up for counsel on making the move.

In all cases, be honest with yourself. The next time you are sitting around the table at a departmental meeting, scrutinize your peers. Ask yourself some questions:

- Are you better than they are?
- If not, can you *become* better than they are?
- If not, can you plan smarter than they can?
- If not, will you be content remaining behind them?
- If not, isn't it time to start planning a move?

PASSED OVER

Every time one of your peers is promoted and you are not, take heed. It does not matter if the promotion is a substantive one, to a new job with a big raise, or a symbolic one, where a new title is awarded but nothing else changes. Either way, a signal has been sent. Someone is making it, and others are not.

Do not gloss over such events or rationalize them away. Don't shrug and say, "Oh, well, I am just too young." Or "I didn't get it because they wanted a woman in that job." Or "I didn't get it because they *didn't* want a woman in that job." It is possible that you failed to get the promotion for a trivial or temporary reason. But you cannot afford to rely on that assumption. You must assume that you were deliberately bypassed, that a conscious decision was made not to promote you—and you have to find out why.

First, consult the corporate tom-toms. Plug into the grapevine and learn everything you can. Why did so-and-so get the new title? Why didn't you? Get as close to the source as you can, whether it is the personnel director or the assistant to the executive who made the decision.

Then go to the horse's mouth. Go see your boss, or whoever it was who made the promotion decision. Ask him or her, "Why didn't I get this job?"

Many people are afraid to do this. They acquiesce in the corporate conspiracy of silence, because they are afraid of what they might hear. Even if the news is bad, you are always better off knowing it than not knowing it. You cannot do anything to improve your situation unless you know what your situation is.

So go see your boss, even if you fear that doing so is on

the brash side of "acceptable" behavior. You are entitled to know how you stand. You deserve to know what you can do to help yourself. You need to know if you have a future. So ask the question. But be prepared for the answer.

It may well be that you were passed over for promotion for reasons that are temporary and pose no threat to your future career. But you may have been passed over for more damaging reasons, reasons that are unlikely to go away. Find out, as specifically as you can, what the reason was in your case, and then act accordingly:

1. "You are too young (or inexperienced)."

No sweat. This is a problem that will take care of itself. Just get back to work. The next promotion may be yours.

2. "You aren't good enough."

Bad news. If your boss truly believes that, you must determine if there is anything you can do that will change his mind. If not, you have got to get the heck out, unless you will be content just to sit at your desk and collect your pay every two weeks for the rest of your life.

3. "It is not convenient for the company to promote you at the moment, because we have nobody to replace you in your current position."

Groom a replacement. Keep your superiors well posted about his or her promising development.

4. "You are too old, too thin, too fat, too short."

None of these attributes (with the possible exception of weight) are changeable. Reconcile yourself to never being promoted, or get out.

5. "You wear the wrong-color suits; your hair is too long; you work too few hours; you work too *many* hours."

You have failed to understand the corporate culture. Get in step. It is not too late.

6. "The company wanted to bring in somebody new from the outside to inject some fresh thinking into the operation."

You are probably okay, but start doing some fresh

thinking yourself. What new and creative ideas do *you* have for improving the business?

7. "You are perfectly well qualified, but no one was really aware of your talents and your desire for the promotion."

You are not packaging yourself effectively, and you are not sufficiently visible. Remember, doing good work is only half of what's required to move up. Your boss, and your boss's boss, must *know* you are doing good work.

8. "You don't have the right kind of experience."

Get it. If your company is promoting only marketing people to group jobs, and you want to be a group executive but you are in finance or production, do not ignore the warning signal. Do not simply sit and hope that next time, a finance person will get the nod. Confirm the preference for marketing people by talking to those who make the promotion decisions. Then make a lateral move, or do whatever you have to, to get some marketing experience. Ditto if you are on the controller side of the finance department and people with treasury skills are being promoted. Or you are a brand manager, and sales people are being promoted. Watch for those trends.

In sum, being passed over for a promotion can be a signal to change your career path, to change your job, or to do nothing at all, depending on the circumstances. In any case, it is a time for self-evaluation.

Richard Braddock, now the head of Citicorp's huge Individual Bank, which includes all the company's consumer banking services, was a senior marketing executive for Citicorp's New York branches when the company was reorganized and the Individual Bank was created in the mid-1970s. Braddock hoped to get one of the senior jobs in the new division, but he was passed over.

"I was in marketing," he recalls. "[Citicorp chairman] John Reed has always described [consumer banking] as a business to be run with a marketing orientation. But in the early days, a lot of these businesses, since they were consumer businesses run in a traditional bank, had been

undernourished managerially. When they were all put together in a pile, it was not the prettiest-looking pile
you've ever seen. So [Reed put] managers in the senior
jobs who by and large had an operations orientation and a
control orientation.... I could understand his logic [for
not picking me], because I didn't have the operations
background and the control orientation—but on the
other hand, there were one or two exceptions in there.
People with my type of background got senior jobs, and I
did not. So I looked at it as basically a negative signal."

Braddock analyzed the situation and saw trouble. "I had
a question as to how quickly they would get into putting
senior marketing people in senior jobs, and I had a question about how fast my career would advance." Braddock
considered leaving the bank, but the bank came to him
and offered him his choice of two new jobs. One was to
become chief of staff to John Reed, then running the consumer banking operation. Braddock was aware, however,
that in a staff position "there was a severe risk that the
job would be a window of underutilization."

Braddock's other alternative was to take over a finance
company Citicorp owned in the United Kingdom. "It was
a very small business and was effectively bankrupt,"
Braddock recalls. He took that job and turned the company around. This gave him the hard-core operations experience he had lacked, and put him firmly on the track
to the top. "I demonstrated in that job in Europe that I
knew how to manage things."

"If I had gotten one of those [senior] jobs [when the
Individual Bank was created], I probably would have done
just fine, but I would have missed the experience of running a bankrupt business back into some semblance of
acceptability, which gave me an understanding that is relatively unique. Many of our senior managers never have
had that kind of experience. Once you have had it, when
the business people come in to talk to you, you know
what they're talking about a lot more than others might.
So whether John had great foresight or not [in not giving
me one of those senior jobs], it was, I think, in hindsight,

better for me to spend my time [running the British business] than just having gotten the brass ring right away."

Braddock drew the correct lesson from being passed over, and he improved his career a great deal as a result.

DO NOT PANIC

If it is fair to conclude that you are fatally blocked—your boss hates you, your employer is going broke, and you are surrounded by brilliant peers—or you have just been passed over for promotion for the third time and have been told that you will be passed over forever, it is obvious that you need to find a new job. But do not rush out and get a new job in a panic. Resist the temptation to take the first new job you can find. The average successful executive changes employers only twice in his career. A hasty job change is likely to be a bad job change.

Being blocked is not the same thing as being fired. Most people who are blocked, even blocked permanently, are never fired. So take your time. Think about your career goals. Seek a job that will move you up toward where you want to go, not one that will merely move you out of a bad situation.

PART 9

CHANGING JOBS

EVERY DAY that you get up and go to work, you have another option: you can quit and go somewhere else. Many people forget that. They live their lives as if they were stuck with their present employer, even though that is rarely true. If you never think about your option of going elsewhere, that doesn't mean that option doesn't exist; it just means that you have decided, by default, that there is no better employer in the world for you than the employer you currently have.

Now, that may be the case. It may be that you are performing well in your present job, and your superiors value you highly, and you are moving nicely up the ladder. Or you may not be moving up, but you like your present rung just fine. There is nothing wrong with saying, "I love my job. This is what I want to do." You may have reached a point where your money needs are satisfied, and your ego needs are satisfied, and you wake up one morning and say to yourself, "Why fuss about going any higher?" One-third of the senior executives in our survey have reached this point; they said they aspire to no higher position than the one they now hold.

If you are happy where you are and wish to stay there, that is fine. But you should make that decision consciously, not for lack of thinking about the subject.

Most people, most of the time, *should* stay where they are. As I discussed earlier, the infatuation some younger executives have with job-hopping is a dangerous delusion. Most successful careers are built by working many years at a single company.

But there are cases when a change is called for. If you are blocked or bored or unhappy, and there is no prospect of an improvement in your situation, you should not be afraid to make a move. The right kind of job change can be the spark that ignites a career.

REASONS FOR MOVING

Every year, Korn/Ferry International approaches thousands of executives and asks them if they are willing to consider a move. If they are happy where they are, they say No, thanks. But a surprisingly large percentage are willing to be pulled away from their current employer. Often, it is because they do not feel they are properly appreciated there.

"It was almost more of an emotional decision than a rational decision," says Norman Blake of his decision to leave General Electric in 1974 and go to a small Detroit company called TOP, Inc. (He returned to G.E. two years later.) "I had a lot of responsibility at G.E. I had several joint ventures reporting to me, and I had people working for me who were making twenty or thirty percent more in base salary than I was. I felt I was not being treated fairly. At the time, I was being sought after by headhunters. Being the Boy Scout that I am, I thought it was very disloyal to consider outside options, so I kept saying no. Ultimately, I went to my boss and said, 'I've never done this before, but it would make a lot of difference to me if you would just give me some recognition from a compensation standpoint.' I remember this conversation vividly. I said, 'It doesn't have to be much; just a little something to say Job well done.' He said, 'I'll see.' And that went on for a couple of months and nothing happened, and I went back, and I got embarrassed.... I really felt like I was not being appreciated. And so I took up this headhunter who had been calling me and calling me and finally I said, 'Yes, I'll talk.' "

The feeling of not being appreciated may result from

insufficient compensation, from conflict with one's boss, from being confined in a job with limited responsibilities or challenges, or from fear of being fired. Some of these are better reasons for moving than others.

Of all of them, the worst single reason to move is money. You should never change jobs *solely* for money, unless it is a great deal of money. It is simply a bad deal, in the long run, to move for a 20-percent raise. People who stay put will catch up with you quickly and very likely eventually pass you by.

In every industry except retailing, low-turnover executives (those who have had one or two employers) earn more money than high-turnover executives (three or more employers) by age forty.

Table 9–1

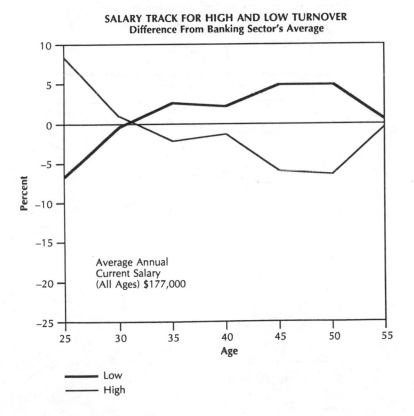

SALARY TRACK FOR HIGH AND LOW TURNOVER
Difference From Banking Sector's Average

Table 9–2

SALARY TRACK FOR HIGH AND LOW TURNOVER
Difference From Insurance Sector's Average

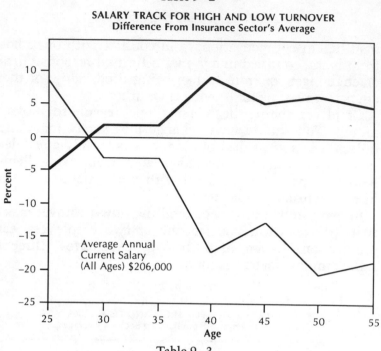

Table 9–3

SALARY TRACK FOR HIGH AND LOW TURNOVER
Difference From Industrial Sector's Average

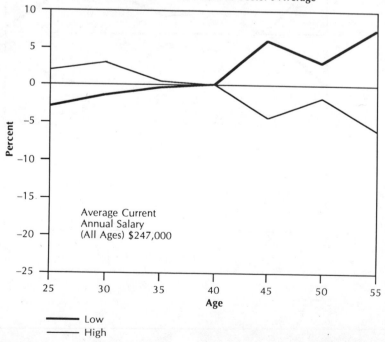

Table 9–4

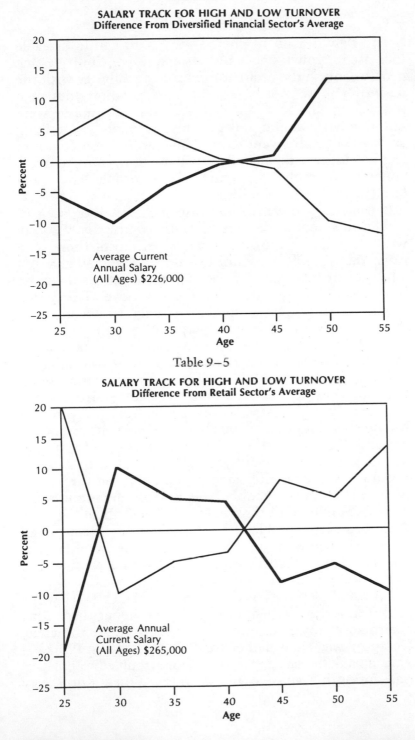

SALARY TRACK FOR HIGH AND LOW TURNOVER
Difference From Diversified Financial Sector's Average

Average Current
Annual Salary
(All Ages) $226,000

Table 9–5

SALARY TRACK FOR HIGH AND LOW TURNOVER
Difference From Retail Sector's Average

Average Annual
Current Salary
(All Ages) $265,000

The right reason to change jobs is to gain a sizeable increase in growth opportunities and responsibility. Some people confuse the desire for more responsibility with the desire for more money. You have to question your own motives in this area. Ask yourself: If more money were not involved, would I want this new job I'm talking about? Do I really want to be challenged? If you do not in fact want more responsibility, you are only going to make yourself miserable by moving to a bigger job (where you face the possibility of failing).

If you truly do want more responsibility, then seek it, and let the money take care of itself. (Eventually, it surely will.) This is the consistent career pattern of those who reach the top. Of the senior executives who had changed jobs, 34 percent cited increased responsibility as the most important factor in their decision to move. Thirty-two percent cited increased challenge. Only 10 percent said their main reason for moving was to gain more pay.

Time and again, the executives I interview talk about the same factors in explaining their own job changes. After setting up a new industry-wide ticketing program at the Air Transport Association, William Waltrip found that simply administering the up-and-running program had no appeal for him. "The challenge had gone out of it," he says. "Eastern Airlines was in the process of trying to overhaul their financial system. They came to me and asked if I would be interested in going there as director of financial systems. Frankly, the Eastern data-processing systems at that point were held together with baling wire. They had a real problem. I saw it as a significant challenge, and as a way to increase my knowledge of the airline industry." (Waltrip eventually became president of Pan American and president of IU International.)

Raymond Dempsey was at a much higher level when Korn/Ferry approached him in 1984 about becoming chairman of the European American Bank. At the time, Dempsey was chairman of the Fidelity Bank in Philadelphia, a bank he had transformed from troubled to prosperous during his six-year tenure there. When Korn/Ferry called him in 1984, Dempsey's first response was no. "I said I had a hell of a deal where I was," he recalls. (During his last year at Fidelity, his total compensation exceeded $1.1 million.)

But Dempsey turned out to be movable, even though the move actually cost him money. "Fidelity had gotten turned around," he explains. "And, very honestly, it began to be boring for me. One thing I've learned about myself is that to run a smooth-running organization is really not interesting to me. I get a kick out of it when I read in magazines that 'the chairman is going to think about strategy.' What the hell do you *do* all day thinking about strategy? That doesn't take twelve hours a day, seven days a week. You'd go crazy." Dempsey was attracted to European American Bank because it was a troubled operation, as Fidelity had been. He took the job.

It is moves like these that lead to career breakouts. Thirty-two percent of the executives we surveyed said that their breakouts resulted from changing employers. Thirty-three percent said they resulted from taking on high-risk projects.

"All of a sudden," says Ray Dempsey, "you get to a level where you say, 'I want more than this... more power, more responsibilities, more tests for myself as a human being.'" Seeking these things, inside or outside one's present company, marks those executives who are destined for the top.

UP OR OUT?

There is more job mobility in America today than in any other major industrial nation. In many countries, job-changing is simply not considered acceptable. In the United States, it is considered natural.

Table 9–6

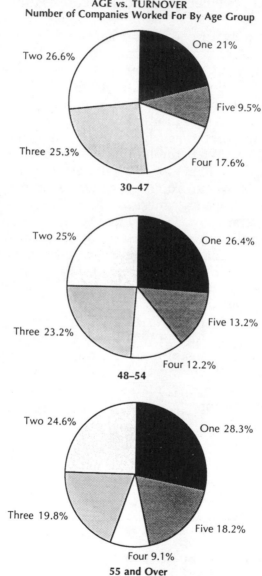

AGE vs. TURNOVER
Number of Companies Worked For By Age Group

Two 26.6%   One 21%

Five 9.5%

Three 25.3%   Four 17.6%

30–47

Two 25%   One 26.4%

Five 13.2%

Three 23.2%   Four 12.2%

48–54

Two 24.6%   One 28.3%

Five 18.2%

Three 19.8%   Four 9.1%

55 and Over

And the job-changing trend is on the rise. Our survey found that the younger an executive is, the less likely it is that he has had only one employer. Twenty-eight percent of those over fifty-five have worked for just one company in their career, compared with 21 percent of those under forty-eight. (Overall, executives switch companies an average of 2½ times in the course of their careers.)

At Korn/Ferry, we make our livings from executive mobility, but we are not in the business of encouraging mobility; we are in the business of making sure that mobility makes sense. It is, in fact, clear to me that there is far too much job-changing going on. As I discussed in Part 3, many job changes are made at the wrong times and for the wrong reasons. People jump to new jobs for relatively small raises that will, in the long run, evaporate. And they jump to jobs that are inappropriate for their career development, because they have failed to give sufficient thought to where they want to go and what they need to accomplish to get there.

Taking a series of jobs is like taking a series of spouses. The more often you get married (or change jobs), the less chance each succeeding marriage (or job) has of working out. Moreover, too much job-hopping simply looks bad and eventually makes highly mobile (and often quite capable) executives unattractive to prospective employers. "You do not want somebody with lack of staying power, or a tendency to give up when there is an apparent block in the way," says Thornton Bradshaw, who headed both Arco and RCA. "There is something to pugnacity and a bulldog quality of getting through obstacles instead of giving up at the first sign of an obstacle. If I see somebody who has been changing jobs every two years, I would regard that as a bad sign."

The first place to look for a better job is within your own company. Faced with a block, the first question to ask yourself is "How can I overcome that block?," not "How do I get out of here?" Eighty percent of all job promotions are made from within; companies don't like to look outside for candidates, and they don't do it unless they have to. A majority of the best careers are based on longevity within a corporation. So I am always shocked at how often executives fail to look for opportunities within their own companies. By all means, look up before you look out. Determine what vacancies will be opening up in your present company during the next two years. (This is something that people are usually willing to talk about. Ask your boss, "Where do you think the company will be in two years?") Ask yourself: Is one of the prospective openings in a position that I can reasonably aspire to? Would getting that job resolve the discontent I feel in my present position? Does my company consider me promotable?

Only if the answers to those questions are no should you look outside. But if they are no, you *should* look outside. It makes no sense to sit and wait in your present job if you have no reasonable prospects for moving up. There are too many over-forty clubs around the country that bear witness to that. If you are hopelessly blocked—or an outside job opportunity comes along that would move you significantly upward in responsibility—go for the change. I only want to emphasize that decisions to change jobs should not be taken lightly, and should be taken only after alternatives within one's present company are explored.

ONE GOOD JOB CHANGE

Some *good* reasons for changing jobs are illustrated in a move Roger Enrico made in 1971. It was a move that met all the criteria for getting out and going somewhere else.

Today, Enrico is president of Pepsi-Cola and a hero of its cola wars with Coke (chronicled in Enrico's book, *The Other Guy Blinked*). But in 1971 he was a twenty-seven-

year-old employee of General Mills. After nine months as
a marketing assistant on Gold Medal Flour, he had just
been made an assistant brand manager of Wheaties. "I
had made the big time," he recalls. "Breakfast cereals are
where it's at at General Mills. But after about six weeks
on the new job, I noticed one little thing was missing. I
had received three biweekly paychecks, and no increase.
So I went in to see the product manager, and I said,
'Didn't I just get promoted?' And he said, 'Yes.' I said,
'Nobody has told me about a raise.' He said, 'That doesn't
make any sense. I'll check into it.' And shortly after that,
he took me into the marketing director's office. The guy
looked at me and he said, 'When we are ready to give you
a raise, we will damned well let you know.' And that
really set me off.... I figured, 'There is something wrong
here.'"

Shortly thereafter, Enrico did get his raise. "The paper-
work was just slow in coming, or something like that....
This guy [who had told me off] was just a jerk. But he
kind of made the bubble burst. I didn't walk out the door
that day. But from that point on I could feel myself slip-
ping. I just didn't have the enthusiasm or the energy any
longer. And I said to myself, 'If I keep this up, my work is
going to suffer, and they'll end up firing me. This is ridiculous.'"

Enrico, as it happened, already had two other reasons
for feeling demoralized. When he had gone to work as a
marketing assistant at Gold Medal Flour, he was paid significantly less than the other marketing assistants, because he did not have an MBA. He thought this unfair,
since those being paid more than he were new employees,
fresh out of school, while he had previously worked at
General Mills (in personnel) before leaving for a stint in
the Navy. But his previous experience and record counted
for nothing. All that mattered in determining the pay
scale was his lack of a graduate degree. "I was the only
junior marketing guy who didn't have an MBA," he says,
"and that was always in the back of my mind.

"And there was something else going on at General

Mills at the time. From a career standpoint, the place was literally beginning to stagnate. I really didn't have to worry about it at the moment, but as I looked forward, I could see it. At that time General Mills was the kind of company that did not let anybody go. Which meant that performance and promotions and compensation did not go as tightly hand in hand as I thought they should. I could see that some of the better people were beginning to bail out and go on to greener pastures. Even the brand-manager slots were blocked. Things were blocked, while there were better people sitting and waiting in the wings to get the positions."

So Enrico faced up to some very tough facts: he had a problem in that he lacked an MBA in a corporate culture that placed a high value on having one; his opportunities for promotion were limited; and all of that was making him unhappy.

"So I just looked in the Yellow Pages to see who the recruiting companies were, and I sent my résumé out to them."

Some time later, one of those companies called him and asked if he'd be interested in working for a snack-foods company in Dallas. It was Frito-Lay, a subsidiary of Pepsico.

"The job there was associate brand manager, which, despite the slight difference in title, was a lateral move. They were going to pay me a little more money, but it was not any big deal at all. I was going to work on an onion-flavored snack called Funyons. It was a dinky brand, but that was not important. The important thing was that this was an entry point into what looked to me like one hell of an opportunity.

"A couple of things struck me about Frito-Lay. Number one was that I could remember all their advertising campaigns without having done any research. The Frito Bandito, and 'I bet you can't eat just one,' and things like that. And I thought, 'God, somebody down there knows something about advertising.' When I got there, I asked them how much money they spent on advertising. And it was unbelievably small compared with the money we were used to spending at General Mills. And I thought, 'Somebody here *really* knows about advertising.'

"I also saw that there were not that many people in the marketing department. I don't think there were twenty. But some of the folks, three or four of them, were damned good. And that was very important, because I needed to learn. The other ten or fifteen were clearly not modern marketing types. They were the old version of marketing guys. Maybe they could put out a promotion for a free pack of bubble gum in the bags. But they could not strategically direct the marketing of brands. And Frito-Lay was just beginning to brand-manage its brands.

"So I said to myself, 'At least three or four of these people can teach me something about marketing. And this company is doing extremely well, and is likely to do even better, in a market that is growing like a bat out of hell. Someday this place is going to be just like General Mills. There are going to be two hundred people in marketing and too much bureaucracy. But I won't care, because I'll be the head of marketing.'"

This was an audacious assumption—that Enrico would learn what he needed to know from the best people at Frito-Lay and that he would leapfrog the rest.

"And that turned out to be exactly right. In less than eight months, my immediate boss left, and I was promoted to his job, running Funyons and Chitos and a whole bunch of other products. And one year after that I was brand manager of Fritos. And a year after that I was marketing director for several hundred million dollars' worth of business. I had Fritos and Doritos and Ruffles and all the corn products—all of the products that made a profit."

Enrico had had solid reasons for leaving General Mills and excellent reasons for joining Frito-Lay. He did not act without thinking, or quit General Mills in a fit of pique. On the contrary, his job move made perfect sense in every way. And it paid off big. He hasn't changed employers since.

CHANGING INDUSTRIES

The hardest job changes to make are those from one industry to another. When a toy manufacturer is looking for a marketing executive, it generally ends up hiring a marketing person from another toy company. If it goes outside its own industry at all, it will probably go to one with common elements—toy retailing, perhaps, or cosmetics or packaged goods. It is not going to consider an aerospace engineer.

Inter-industry job moves are best accomplished young. It is not unusual for young people to more or less bumble into their first jobs. If you have bumbled into yours, decide as fast as you can if you like it. If not, jump industries while you're still young enough to go in at an entry-level position.

"I started working as an engineer for Standard Oil of California," recalls James Harvey, the chairman of Transamerica Corporation, "and I enjoyed it. But I looked around and saw a heck of a lot of other great people working as engineers and that it would take me forever to work my way up in the engineering field. I also felt confined by engineering. I had friends who were stockbrokers and investment bankers who were involved in all kinds of interesting things. They were kind of living in the real world, and I was behind a fence in an oil refinery." Harvey took a leave of absence and went to business school.

Albert Snider, former president of Bourns, Inc., is another engineer-turned-businessman. As a young man, he found himself working with several distinguished scientists in the field of nuclear engineering. "I found I wasn't able to perform at the level I wanted to perform....I would sit there with those guys, and I saw that inanimate metal objects *talked* to them. They could just *see* what else could be done, and I had to talk to somebody to find out what else could be done. I am a human-instinct person as opposed to an engineering person. So I got out and went to Harvard Business School, and I have never been happier with any other major decision."

What we're dealing with here is basically a case of "know thyself." It's hard enough to succeed in a line of work that you enjoy. It's just about impossible to succeed in a field where you feel you don't really belong. Your feelings are, in fact, a key part of the analysis. If what you're doing doesn't feel right, get out while you have the chance. Trust your instincts.

In 1968, Donald Beall left Ford's aerospace-electronics subsidiary for Rockwell International, where he is now CEO. "To get to the top at Ford," he says, "you have to be in the automotive business. I did not want to be in the automotive business. I did not want to be in any single-product business. I knew that I would be more likely to be happy, and indeed more likely to fare well, if I were in a diversified, high-technology business." It was a good call. Beall thrived in just such a world at Rockwell.

Beall's shift from Ford to Rockwell was not an enormous leap; he was already working in high technology and he had been trained as an engineer. Often, critical mid-career industry changes involve only subtle shifts in what one is doing, or where one is doing it. Both William Smithburg, chairman of Quaker Oats, and Philip Smith, head of General Foods, were successful advertising men when they decided to move into marketing jobs in the companies they now run. The step from advertising to marketing is a short one, but for Smithburg and Smith, it was crucial. It put them in places where they felt they belonged, and thus put them on the road to success.

"In the advertising-agency business," Smithburg recalls, "I'd work days and nights and weekends, and I'd make recommendations to my clients. And they would pat me on the back and say, 'Good job. Excellent presentation.' And then I would go back two months later and I would say, 'What ever happened to this idea?' And they would say, 'Well, we decided not to do that.' Finally, I decided I had to be where I could make those decisions. I did not want to be a professional recommender."

"The real decision power lies with clients," Smith concurs. "So if you discover that you like to control your environment, and you like to be the person who decides what it is you're going to do, once you come to that realization you decide, 'I'm not going to be in the agency business. I'm going to work for a manufacturer.'"

Some of the most publicized inter-industry job moves in recent years have occurred at the highest levels. Top executives have moved to companies in seemingly very different industries, leaving the general public wondering how a soft-drink man, for example, could possibly know anything about computers. In these cases, apparent differences are often deceiving. John Sculley moved from Pepsico to Apple Computer not because he knew anything about floppy-disk drives—he didn't need to; plenty of people at Apple know all there is to know about floppy-disk drives—but because he had proved experience in consumer marketing, and that is what Apple, founded by brilliant technical entrepreneurs, needed.

If specific experience in a job like the one to be filled is crucial, then we at Korn/Ferry could never have found anyone to head the Los Angeles Olympic Organizing Committee. How many candidates were there kicking around who had previously run an Olympics? To guide our search, we enumerated the elements of the Olympics job. We ended up seeking someone who was interested in sports, who was successful in a service industry, who was a good communicator, who had a strong finance and planning background, who understood the logistics of moving large numbers of people around, who knew how to make a profit. When we added all those up, it seemed we ought to have a look into travel and related industries. We did, and found Peter Ueberroth, then running First Travel, the nation's second-largest travel-services organization.

Ueberroth's move was an inter-industry job change that

made sense—if you thought about it. Like all such mid-career moves, it could work only if there was some kind of logic to it, obvious or not.

FROM LAW INTO MANAGEMENT

Lawyers are plentiful in the top ranks of American corporations, but some of them are running the companies while others are still just...lawyers.

As I discussed earlier, one cannot reach the top in American business without breaking out of the "staff syndrome." Corporate lawyers are corporate staffers. If they never do anything but legal work, then, with rare exceptions, legal work is all they will ever do. Many are perfectly happy with that situation and have fine careers, reaching levels as high as vice president/general counsel. But those who want to break out of lawyering must be aware that they need, at some point, to get profit-center responsibility and to build a track record of putting dollars on the bottom line.

There is an obvious Catch-22 here. If you are a lawyer who wants to break out of legal work, how do you get the general-management experience you need to get your first general-management job?

First of all, you lift your head out of your legal work. "If a lawyer is going to 'overlawyer' everything to death, he is probably going to stay a lawyer," says Douglas McCorkindale, an attorney who is vice chairman of the Gannett media empire. "If he wants to become a manager, he has to learn how to apply his legal thinking process, which is basically logical analysis, to other problems. If he just keeps the legal blinders on, and always deals with only the legal aspects of a problem or transaction, he will stay within that narrow confine. He should look at the bigger picture, and worry about the personnel aspects, and the financial aspects, and the public relations aspects."

Fine, but what if you are a lawyer who is willing and able to see the big picture, but simply don't have the opportunity to do so in your present job?

Then you have the wrong kind of *law* job. A prerequisite of moving from law to general management seems to be having the right kind of legal position from which to make your move.

"I was not a legal practitioner with just those narrow confines," says McCorkindale, who was a Wall Street lawyer for seven years before he joined Gannett in 1971. "I was what you might call a 'deal lawyer' on the Street back in the 1960s. There was a great boom then of mergers and acquisitions and people going public. And I just happened to be the right guy in the right spot in that particular law firm. I was handling the legal *and* the financial side of some of my clients' affairs. I had a number of job offers to go with investment-banking firms, because I was doing those sorts of things." Instead, McCorkindale joined Gannett. "I came here as general counsel, but also to do the acquisition work. Gannett was looking for someone who was 'a lawyer,' but who also understood the business side of doing transactions."

One way to start learning business, McCorkindale says, is to get involved with one's clients' businesses. (As a prerequisite, one must be in the type and size of law firm where that is possible.) "If, as a client, you get a lawyer who is working with you day in and day out on transactions, and he does his legal job but also starts providing additional advice, comments, and counsel when you go out to dinner, he can broaden his horizons."

Something like this happened to Marshall Manley, a brilliant lawyer and strategist who is president of The Home Group, Inc., and chairman of its subsidiary The Home Insurance Company. Previously he was a partner and chairman of the management committee of Finley,

Kumble, Wagner, Heine, Underberg, Manley, Myerson & Casey, then one of the nation's largest law firms. In 1985, Manley became president of City Investing Company, which was then voluntarily liquidating and from which Home Insurance was about to be spun off. "For twenty-some years, I had been one of the important attorneys for City Investing," Manley says. "During that period, I assume because of what I did and how I interacted with the management of City Investing, they began to like the way I thought and my attitude toward business. When it came time to do the voluntary liquidation, I was brought in as president because it involved not only managerial skills but also a knowledge of the legal process."

And Manley had both—legal knowledge and managerial skills. He joined Finley Kumble when it had forty-seven lawyers and played a major role in building it to a firm of more than five hundred lawyers. "As a managing partner of one of the largest law firms in the country in those years, I had a great deal of responsibility to make sure we made money," Manley points out. So he had on-the-job management training—as a lawyer.

Manley is a multitalented achiever who is likely to become one of those keystone executives who will shape American business policy over the next two or three decades. He made a substantial mark in every law firm he ever worked for, and he is doing great things for Home today. In addition, like other successful executives, he serves on the boards of civic and cultural organizations. "I find it very difficult when somebody asks me how I break down my time," he says. "I do everything full time."

The final step in moving from law to management is joining the right kind of company when you are ready to make your move. When McCorkindale went to Gannett, it was small but growing. "We did nineteen newspaper acquisitions in the first nineteen months I was there," he recalls. There was plenty of room for everybody to take on new responsibilities.

Also, partly because it was still relatively small, Gannett was the kind of company in which labels like "lawyer" did not matter. The structure was loose enough to enable talented, ambitious people to make of their careers what they could.

"The way Gannett is structured," McCorkindale says, "we do not put people in boxes. It is not like IBM or AT&T. When you are at a certain level in Gannett, you all get involved in the business operations. You tend to take on responsibilities.... When I came here, I was the company's lawyer and their acquisitions guy. I was also responsible for real estate, and I sort of looked after television. We owned a couple of stations, and it sort of came to me because nobody else was responsible for it. The chief financial officer left in 1975, so I took over that. We continued to grow, and I ended up running several divisions."

In sum, lawyers who move successfully into management need to seek the kinds of broad-focus legal jobs that will give them a chance to hone their general business skills and then to join the kinds of companies where they will be given the opportunity to spread their wings. Such law jobs, and such companies, are identifiable, if one is willing to do some homework. Talk to past and present employees, study the financial and legal press, read annual reports and financial documents. This all takes time, but the investment is a necessary one for lawyers who want to break out of the staff syndrome.

This same prescription, with minor adjustments, applies to personnel executives, financial executives, and other executives with staff functions. Very few senior executives start out in general management. But they make a point of getting there.

THE INDEPENDENT
ALTERNATIVE

If you have concluded that you must get out of your present job, before you look for a different one consider another option: going off on your own. Ask yourself if your frustration in your current position isn't perhaps a result of being in a large company.

It was for me. At the age of thirty-two, I made up my mind to leave the lifetime security of a partnership in the accounting firm of Peat Marwick to found Korn/Ferry International with Dick Ferry, my friend and partner at Peat Marwick. My dissatisfaction with company life had begun to crystallize a few years before. When I was twenty-nine, I had earned a partnership but was told I would have to wait a year to get one because of the then-ironclad rule No Partnerships Before Thirty. I asked myself, "Is this the way it's going to be?" and I concluded, "Yes, it probably is." I preferred to be the master of my own destiny.

I understood that that decision meant I might be dining on hamburger for the rest of my days. Starting a business is an immense gamble and, almost invariably, requires far more work than any job does. But it was something I needed to do. Fortunately, we succeeded.

One of the best-planned independent ventures I have ever encountered is that of Fred Malek, who is today executive vice president of the Marriott Corporation. After graduating from Harvard Business School in 1964, Malek went to work at the prestigious consulting firm of McKinsey & Company, but he already had a secret plan for independence. "Before I graduated from business school," Malek says, "a group of us got together and

began to have periodic meetings to try to find a way that
we, as a group, could buy a company. That was our stated
ambition. After we got jobs, we continued this with a
kind of subterfuge. We worked on it nights and weekends,
as time permitted. And we met quarterly.

"We would actually have assignments. We would pick
out certain industries that we thought were hot, and we
would go out and investigate them. We finally decided
that mobile homes was the way to go. So we would go out
on nights and weekends to mobile-home parks and interview people. We applied the Harvard Business School analytical approach to why these people bought mobile
homes, and what they were looking for, and what they
liked about the products they had, and what they didn't
like.

"We had selected one guy to be our leader, and he was
going to quit his job and go full time into the mobile-
home industry and work there for a period of time, so that
we would have some industry perspective before we
bought a mobile-home company. But just at the time he
was going to make his move—he had an offer from a
mobile-home company—he more or less got drafted by
the Defense Department. . . .

"That sort of broke the group apart. Two of us were out
in southern California, and we decided we would go in
together, and we recruited a third guy, who knew manufacturing. It took us a year to make a major decision: that
somebody had to work full time at this. We drew straws,
and the guy with the short straw quit his job and worked
full time finding a company to buy. The other two of us
pooled our salaries, and we split them three ways.

"The guy who quit his job found a company called the
Utica Tool Company in Orangeburg, South Carolina, and
we bought it for nine million dollars. The three of us put
up fifty thousand, which was all we had between us. And
for that, we got about twenty-five percent of the company.

"We had put together a group of equity investors. Here
we were, three energetic young guys out there trying to

lick the world. And that was a time when there was a general feeling that bright people could accomplish any-thing—unlike today, when you really want people with industry experience.

"Our investors put up $1.95 million, to bring our eq-uity to two million dollars. And we borrowed seven mil-lion dollars. Four and a half million was against the assets of the company, and $2.5 million was taken back by the seller in a note.

"I quit my job and moved to South Carolina. I was chairman. There were three of us, and we were all co—chief executives. Two of us moved to Orangeburg to run the company, which we renamed the Triangle Corpora-tion, and the third guy moved to New York, on the theory that it only took two of us to run the company and we needed somebody to work on new acquisitions."

Malek and his friends were brought down to earth for a while by unexpected difficulties. "If we had known every-thing we later learned, we probably would not have bought the company. Once we got in there, the situation was a lot worse than we had thought. We had not ana-lyzed it thoroughly or correctly."

Nevertheless, within two years they had turned the company around. "It just took a lot of perseverance, a lot of getting in there and just doing the basics well. My partner and I shared an office and we rode to work to-gether. We would leave our houses at seven o'clock in the morning and we would seldom get home before nine o'clock at night. Half the time I was traveling, rebuilding our distribution. It was a pretty tough existence."

Malek and his partners not only got Triangle back on track; they actually did go on to make some acquisitions. "We bought two other companies that we folded in with Triangle, and we went public. We were moving along at a good pace. By 1969, the market value of my stock was two million dollars—it had a very high multiple. My partners put together a group that offered me a little over one million dollars for it. In my naïveté, I thought it really was worth two million, so I didn't take the offer. It was a big mistake. I sold about a hundred thousand dollars' worth to buy a house, and I finally sold the rest of it in 1984 for four or five hundred thousand."

Still, not a bad result for such an audacious venture, and Malek emerged with a growing reputation.*

Malek quit Triangle in 1969, by the way, to take a political job in Washington, something few business people ever do. (Fewer than 2 percent of senior executives have ever taken a leave of absence for government service.)

The general lack of interest in government jobs is a loss to the country, but probably not a loss to most executive careers. "While government experience adds a certain breadth and understanding you cannot get any other way, I think it is probably more of an interruption to a career in business than an augmentation to such a career," says Malek.

For Malek himself, government service was a career roller coaster. He spent five years in the Nixon administration, including three as special assistant to the president. Immediately after the 1972 election, he reports, "I had some excellent opportunities. I was very much sought after." Following the Watergate scandal (in which Malek played no part), he was less in demand. "Coming out of the Nixon administration at that time was not the greatest reference." (Times change. Today it is!)

Malek believes, and I concur, that having some government service in your background is a definite plus when you are being considered for senior executive positions; but taking time off to get that government experience may, by interrupting your career, make it harder to reach the level where you would be considered for such jobs in the first place.

---

*His two partners did pretty well too. One of them, Art Bellows, is still the chairman of Triangle. The other, Warren Bass, is chairman of Premark International, which spun off from Dart and Kraft in 1986.

THE JOB HUNT

When you reach the conclusion that you ought to leave your present job and find another one, the first thing to do is: nothing. That is, do not act rashly. Do not get angry, tell your boss "I quit!" and march out the door into an unknown future. Even if you are mad as hell, keep yourself under control. It is time to start *looking for* another job; it is not time to resign. (It is, by the way, almost never time to "resign" as a bargaining tactic with your current employer. People who have tried it with me over the years have learned this lesson. When someone, even someone very good, tells me he is quitting, I do not say, "Are you sure? Is there anything we can do about it?" I just shake his hand and tell him it has been very nice having him around and proceed to an amicable parting.)

It takes some time, up to a couple of years, to position yourself to make a move. The first step is self-evaluation. How do you stand within your present company? Are there any slots opening up there that you would be qualified for that are compatible with your career goals? What do you need to do next in your career? What do you want to do?

If the answers to these questions lead you to look at other companies, then make a research project of it. Follow the trade papers. Check the employment ads. Talk to competitors. Look for companies that suit your needs at the same time you can suit theirs. Meanwhile, give such companies a look at you by attending industry meetings, making speeches, working on industry committees and generally making yourself visible in every way you can.

SELLING YOURSELF

When the time comes to find a new job, look at yourself as something to be sold. Face the cold, hard fact that you are a product. Be that product's brand manager. Figure out what skills and experience you have to offer, and define the market for those skills and that experience. What companies, what divisions within those companies, can really use an experienced financial analyst who speaks Spanish, or a systems engineer with knowledge of micro-computers and cattle ranching? (Consider also whether you would be significantly more marketable if you held off changing jobs for a year or two and used that time to gain some additional skills or experience within your present company.)

If you are still in the first part of your career, third par-ties like headhunters are not likely to be of much use to you. Major search firms deal only with senior executives and are not very much interested in people earning less than $75,000 a year. This does not mean that employers are not looking for people like you. It just means that they are probably conducting their searches themselves. It is up to you to bring yourself to their attention.

You may do this indirectly, through industry network-ing, or do it very directly, by writing a letter to some-one you would like to work for. If you are a disgruntled employee in the corporate-finance department of one investment-banking firm, there is nothing wrong with writing a letter to the corporate-finance department of another. Address it to the line executive in charge of the area, or even to the president. Even if it doesn't get you a job, it may get you an interview.

Such a letter should be kept short (two pages at most) and ought to make three points:

1. That you are interested in talking with the executive about career opportunities within his or her com-pany.

2. That you would like your inquiry to remain confidential.

3. That you have done certain things which merit the attention of his or her company. List your title, your responsibilities, and what you have accomplished.

You should not indicate what kind of salary you are seeking—you don't want to take the chance of pricing yourself too low—but you should put down your present compensation (salary plus bonus). This goes against the grain for many people, but it is a good way to avoid wasting everybody's time. If the person to whom you are writing is looking for a $200,000 person, he will probably not deal with you if you are earning only $60,000. You are just in a different league. If he has an $80,000 job, and you are earning $100,000, he will know not to waste your time.

Job-seeking letters may be shotgunned to dozens or even hundreds of companies simultaneously. Known as "broadcast letters," these amount to informal mini-résumés (do not include your formal résumé). The letters should be one page long and addressed to chief executive officers. Identify yourself and list your accomplishments. (Even if you are new to the work force, you have some accomplishments. "I spent last summer managing a snack bar and sales went up 65 percent over the previous year.") Say that you would like to work for the addressee's company, and say why. The theory here is that somebody, somewhere, is looking for somebody like you, and you just might find him.

Such letters really do work. Gary Wilson, the executive vice president of Disney, sent out "hundreds" of them, he says, when he was looking for a financial position in 1973. (He had previously been chief financial officer of the Trans-Philippines Investment Company and executive vice president of Checchi & Company, a consulting firm.) "I got lots of replies, lots of interviews," he says. His letter arrived on the desk of Marriott Corporation chairman Bill Marriott just when the company was looking for a treasurer. Marriott sent the letter down to his chief financial officer with a note to check Wilson out. Coincidentally, the accounting firm that audited both Checchi and Marriott recommended Wilson to the chief financial officer at about the same time. Wilson is convinced that both the letter and the recommendation helped him get the job.

If there is a specific company that you know you want to work for, then go for it and let out all the stops. In 1954, Harry Gray, who later became one of America's business superstars, was employed at Greyvan Lines, a division of Greyhound. Gray decided he wanted to work at then brand-new Litton Industries. He was impressed with the company's founders, he expected it to grow, and he was aware of and attracted by its innovative stock-option plan. Moreover, he had determined that "there was nobody in that group who had real commercial experience," so he thought Litton could use him. He launched a campaign to get a job there.

"What most impressed me [about Gray] was not his journalism degree or his experience with Greyvan," Litton cofounder Roy Ash (who later became Director of the Office of Management and Budget) recalled thirty years later, "but I've never seen anyone make a more thoroughly planned or effectively carried-out job application. In the days before his arrival we received letters recommending him. On the day he arrived he caused me and Tex [Thornton] to receive three or four phone calls about him from our bankers and such. When he arrived, we knew he wanted that job. We thought we could use him."

"I found out who their bankers were," Gray confirms, "and I found a way to get introduced to them. A friend of mine who was at a bank in the Midwest knew a senior officer at Litton's bank. I had that banker and his assistant interview me in great detail, and we spent a lot of time together. It was good chemistry, and they recommended me."

Gray also found time to design and print a custom résumé. "Having been involved in advertising, I knew something about layout and graphics. I wanted it to be

simple. It was an attractive light gray color with my
name printed on the front in blue ink, very pleasing just
to look at. It made you want to open it to see what was on
the first page. The paper was a very nice bond. Everything
was printed, so the lines were short to read. At the bottom of every page I had a gray stripe to lead you onto the
next page. You could go through the whole darn thing in
two minutes, and you'd know everything.... I wanted to
have something attractive. The only product I had to sell
was me."

RÉSUMÉS AND INTERVIEWS

In describing oneself in interviews and résumés, there is a
natural tendency to embellish. Yes, one should put the
best face on one's past. But no, one should never lie, or
even exaggerate.

Not long ago, Korn/Ferry conducted a search for a city
manager. The leading candidate indicated that he had two
university degrees he turned out not to have. He was
eliminated from consideration as a result of that foolish
and unnecessary lie. The city had wanted him. If he *had*
had the degrees he claimed, it would have been irrelevant.
He was at a stage of life where his work experience more
than compensated for any lack of formal education. This
kind of disaster is avoidable—by honesty. (To avoid inad-
vertent disaster, keep records of your credentials. A care-
less clerk or a college office might make a mistake when
a reference-checker calls. Be prepared to unscramble mix-
ups quickly.)

Job candidates often claim credit for things their bosses,
or their subordinates, have done. ("So many people have
claimed to be the father of the Mustang that I wouldn't
want to be seen in public with the mother," Lee Iacocca
has noted.) This too is bad practice and generally doomed
to failure. Do not say you were responsible for marketing
a successful new product if it wasn't really you but one of
your colleagues who did it. A potential employer, in
checking your references, will discover the truth, and that

will be the end of you. If you had been honest, the fact that you even were part of the team that implemented the product introduction might have been enough to get you the job. Your potential new employer probably couldn't get the person who was directly responsible for the product's success; by participating, you had a valuable experience.

Job candidates also sometimes claim to *be* their bosses. Don't fiddle with your titles. If you were Supervisor of Data Processing, don't promote yourself to Director of Data Processing. The title is probably irrelevant anyway, but it could suddenly raise an important issue of your credibility.

Your résumé should focus on experiences relevant to the job you seek, but it should omit nothing. If you spent 1975 washing dishes on a tramp steamer and 1976 as a lifeguard, say so (briefly). If, instead, you write "miscellaneous jobs—1975–76," or leave any years unaccounted for, rest assured that's the first thing an interviewer will ask you about. He or she will need to determine that you did not spend those years in a prison or mental institution. You want to make it easy for people to hire you. Filling gaps in incomplete résumés is extra work they may not care to spend time on.

An effective résumé will include a list of tangible achievements for which the applicant can take credit. The best judge of the future is the past; one's résumé should display a successful past. The ideal résumé for a senior position would include the following items. If you are young, you can't possibly have them all on your own record, but you should be making a conscious effort to touch these bases as your career develops:

- a proved profit-and-loss track record
- experience in a turnaround situation with a product or division
- a successful new-product introduction or new market development
- some experience with corporate finance
- a record of developing promising executives.

Interviews are stressful, but keep in mind when you go in for one that you already have a big leg up on all those who were not invited to be interviewed. You have already made a good impression somehow. So you don't have to make a big point of establishing yourself. You don't have to recite your résumé. You can afford to be a little more relaxed, a little more quiet, a little more thoughtful—all of which will make for a better interview.

Calm? Good. Now, here are five key interview rules:

1. Do your homework.

Be prepared. Read the company's annual report. Know what the job is. Talk to people who no longer work for the company, and to people who do. Cram yourself with knowledge about the company and the job. It is far better to be able to say, "You have a wonderful company; I enjoyed reading that article about it in *Fortune* last year," than to have to gulp for air upon being asked, "Why do you want to work for an organization you apparently know nothing about?"

I sat down not long ago with a man who earns more than $2 million a year who was a candidate for president of a major company. He said he knew the company, but had not had time to read the 10-K. I was shocked, but had to be tolerant with a very hot potential candidate for a presidency. Personnel executives will not tolerate a low-level job applicant who says, "I don't really know what Colgate-Palmolive does, but I sure would like to work there."

Your homework should also tell you if you have a realistic chance to get the job you seek. Some employers seek clones of themselves. If they studied engineering at an Ivy League college and then switched to finance, they may think such a background is the best possible business training. If you don't have it, you might be barking up the wrong tree.

2. Don't knock your present company.

Do not display a strong negative attitude toward your current employer. The only major complaint you should have is that you find a lack of upward opportunity there.

Sometimes an interviewer will encounter a candidate with a high level of anger that spills over into everything. The intensity may seem like a high energy level at first, but eventually one finds oneself with a sullen soul who will alienate people instead of motivating them.

3. Be honest.

You ought to be able to state a logical, and true, reason for wanting to leave your present job. If you're coming out of a company or unit that has been unsuccessful, say so, but separate yourself from the failure if you can. If you've made mistakes, be prepared to discuss them. If you had a problem with your boss, say so, without going into the details. There is nothing wrong with a personality clash. Everybody has them.

4. Display confidence.

If you are asked if you honestly think you can handle the job you seek, say "Yes." Don't ask for time to think it over. Nobody wants to hire an uncertain person for a leadership position. You may *be* uncertain, but keep it to yourself.

5. Talk about money last.

One of the games you must learn to play is to act as if salary were not very important to you, even though it probably is. Most job applicants want to start by talking about money. Most employers want to finish there. Go along with them. If they decide they want you for the job, $5,000 more or less isn't going to make much difference to them. You do yourself a favor by waiting. And don't even think about discussing retirement benefits and vacation time until you have a job offer. Interviewers want people who are concerned with doing the job, not getting away from it.

OUT OF WORK

As a recruiter, I run into a lot of euphemisms. People are "thinking about making a change." They "aren't there anymore." They are never "out of a job."

People avoid those words for good reason. Being out of

work is a very sad place to find oneself. Albert Snider, former president of Bourns, Inc. (and now EVP for Avnet), was briefly unemployed in 1973 and recalls it as a time of "acid in the stomach."

"I went out of the house every day and never told my wife I didn't have any place to go. She thought I was going to work. I was going out walking the streets looking for a job....Don't get me wrong. I wasn't going to the park and feeding turtles. I was knocking on doors, visiting people, having lunches, keeping things moving....I don't remember how long this went on. It seemed like an eternity at the time. It was either four or six weeks."

If you have been planning your career wisely, you should never be unemployed. Terminations are rarely personal. They occur because a company is trimming back a division or is in some kind of trouble. These are problems you should be able to foresee, if you study your company and industry as diligently as you should. If terminations are on the horizon, move to another division or company before they occur.

If your termination is unforeseeable, or you simply haven't enough time to get out before it comes, you are in big trouble. The best way to find a job is to have one. Your currency plunges the minute you are unemployed ("After I was fired, it was as if I ceased to exist," wrote Lee Iacocca), and you are likely to be stunned and demoralized.

The instant you are given notice, get to work finding a new job. Do not waste time hoping for a miracle to save you; do not succumb to shell shock. During the notice period, do an immediate evaluation of your skills and make a list of companies that might be able to use them. Include both local companies and those out of town. If you have to look outside your chosen industry or area, do so.

Find out what your present company is going to say about you when asked for a reference. Don't be afraid to ask. It is your right to know, and it can make or break your future.

Call everyone you can think of whom you could possibly work for. Keep in mind that you need a job in thirty days, not sometime next year. In every interview, convey the impression (without sounding desperate) that you are not just browsing in the market, that *this* is the job you want.

HEADHUNTERS

Executive-search firms, commonly known as "head-hunters," are among the most important—and least understood—players in the job-changing process. (Unlike some others in my business, I do not object to the term "headhunters." I might prefer to be called a "distinguished executive-search consultant," but the fact remains that unless I say "headhunter" most people don't know what I'm talking about.)

What many job-seekers fail to understand is that head-hunters do not work for individuals; they work for companies and other entities, which engage them for specific assignments to find qualified people for specific jobs. Companies are the headhunters' clients; individual executives are their "inventory." It may not be flattering to think of yourself as a piece of goods on a headhunter's shelf, but that is what you are.

Or that may be what you *hope* to be. Korn/Ferry and other executive-search firms are flooded daily with unsolicited résumés from individuals who want to become part of our inventory, because they are unhappy in their present jobs and look to us to get them out. The majority of people who write search firms do so in vain. Like other major firms, we deal in executives already earning $100,000 and up. Our clients do not hire us to search for younger, less experienced, less successful individuals.

The search business is booming today. The intensely competitive international business environment has put

unprecedented pressures on American business executives. Corporate managers find themselves operating in a
fishbowl, under floodlights. Bad decisions which in the
past would have been buried in oblivion are now just as
likely to end up on the evening news. Stockholders demand endless successes. Takeover specialists are waiting
in the wings, in case stock prices fail to keep pace with
shareholders' idea of value. Foreign corporations are buying American companies as never before.

Meanwhile, American corporations are transforming
themselves daily. Companies are merging and buying one
another at a dizzying rate. There is also a major, if less
remarked on, trend toward spin-offs and divestitures.
Large companies are evaluating the potential of subsidiary business units; some are being spun off into corporate
lives of their own.

What does all this mean for managers? For some of
them, it means "good-bye." You can see this chronicled
in the "Who's News" column of *The Wall Street Journal*
and similar columns in other publications. There are the
resignations for "early retirement"; for policy reasons;
"to pursue other business interests"; resignations amid
reports of problems, losses, lackluster performance. With
increasing frequency, executives are being squeezed out or
dismissed, or just walking away in frustration. The good
news is: every resignation or dismissal produces an opportunity for someone else.

NO MORE POTTED PLANTS

To replenish their ranks, companies are turning to headhunters at a steadily increasing rate. The "old boy net-
work" is history. Business has become too complicated,
and the stakes too high, for a board chairman who needs
executive talent to rely on his friends or his friends' recommendations.

With the search net being cast wider, corporate leaders
seek the help of professionals. Most corporate executives
are neither very comfortable nor very knowledgeable

about the selection of people. Headhunters simplify managers' lives and increase their comfort factor, while providing a sort of guarantee (to themselves and to outside overseers) that an impartial, systematic search has been conducted.

In performing this valuable service, the search industry has come a long way from its early days, when most outfits were Mom-and-Pop operations and the media pictured searchers as individuals who crouched behind potted plants in building lobbies and called out "Psst, want a good job?" to passing executives. I am proud that Korn/Ferry led the way in such areas as the development of huge computerized data bases, full-time research sections that track thousands of executive careers, specialized in-house "boutiques" that focus on specific industries, and designated account partners who oversee all the worldwide recruitment needs of specific clients (and come to function as their human-resources consultants). In sum, the search business has become a profession.

HOW A SEARCH IS CONDUCTED

A typical search begins with a series of meetings between the hiring company and the searcher. A company may call us and tell us it is looking for a vice president—marketing, but we know there is more to it than that. Before we can begin our job, we need to know not only what the job title will be, but also to whom the person holding the job will report, what the compensation will be, and exactly what the new executive will be expected to *do* to be considered a success. Rudimentary things, but all too often they have not been thought through when the first call to a headhunter goes out.

Eventually, the searcher and company together produce a document that describes the job to be filled and the kind of person sought to fill it. A recent, not atypical, job specification called on us to find a candidate who:

> possesses leadership qualities; is creative and innovative as opposed to reactive; has the capability to very

quickly grasp and understand the present operational capabilities of these units with regard to strategic direction and available resources; has strong interpersonal skills and an ability to recognize that objectives will be achieved mainly through the efforts of others; has the ability to work effectively with the chief executive officer; is an excellent communicator; has demonstrated outstanding leadership capabilities through the start-up or turnaround of a business in the telecommunications equipment industry; whose career path has included a broad exposure to the product system and services of the industry; whose present position is a significant one with responsibility for implementing major operations; is known and respected by the financial community.

And that kind of tall order, which is typical, is usually only part of the story. One recent job description specified: "The individual must be of a stature that commands respect." Sentences like this are often code for "distinguished-looking" or, simply, "tall." The headhunter has to draw out the client's intangible preferences, as the object of a search is not merely to find someone with the right paper credentials, but to find someone who has the credentials and will also fit in. It's a waste of everybody's time and money if we turn up a bearded, no-socks genius for a client who prefers conservative executives in pinstriped suits. And this works both ways. I once recruited a New York executive, accustomed to posh surroundings, for the presidency of a well-regarded but bare-bones West Coast corporation that didn't believe in spending money on such office luxuries as Persian carpets and antique desks. The New Yorker got the job, moved West, and quit at 4 P.M. on his first day. (This was not one of my happiest days. Fortunately, the backup candidate took the job and became a superb president.)

Job description and other criteria in hand, our search partner turns to the resources of our research department. Its first task is to compile a "target list" of companies in the same industry or a closely related industry as the hiring company. The most desirable characteristic a job candidate can have is a proved track record of success in a similar job. Companies don't want to take chances on people. They want proved commodities. The safest hire for a company is someone from one of that company's direct competitors. So that is where we look. (Simultaneously, our computers are pulling résumés of possible candidates.)

Once the target list is compiled, we comb through those companies, looking for those people in positions similar to the position we are seeking to fill. Candidates need not already be at the same level of title and salary. Commonly, they are one level down; the job they get through us is their step up.

When we identify potential candidates, we call them. The old headhunter's line—"We are looking for somebody to fill such-and-such a position. Do you happen to know anybody who might be qualified and interested?"— is still in play. The line is designed to avoid embarrassment. Most of the time the headhunter is hoping for the response "How about me?"

If such a response is not forthcoming, the searcher will persevere. "Well, how about yourself?" If the person answers, "I don't think I qualify," the headhunter will prod at that a little to see if it's true. If the person says, "Not interested," the headhunter will poke at *that* to see if there's any way interest may be aroused.

The headhunter's immediate task, at this point, is to get potential candidates to meet with him (not with the client; not yet). At an initial meeting, the searcher can size up the candidate's interest (it must exist; he came to the interview), his qualifications, the way he presents himself, and whether he or she fits the culture of the hiring corporation.

What follows is a delicate dance. Promising candidates are courted. The hiring company is consulted. The headhunter conducts shuttle diplomacy between them, facilitating negotiations, most often in an atmosphere of strict confidentiality. Candidates for positions like corporate president don't want it to be known—ever—that they were considered, unless they get the job, and corporations often don't like to acknowledge that they have used search firms until the position is filled, if then.

In the end, one candidate is hired. A major career move has been made. And—a new vacancy has been created.

ATTRACTING HEADHUNTERS' INTEREST

One attracts the attention of headhunters the same way one attracts the attention of potential employers or, for that matter, one's boss's boss—by making oneself visible. All of the tactics for gaining visibility I have already discussed apply here. The research departments of search firms read and clip financial and trade papers. Do something to get yourself mentioned, and you will end up in the major headhunters' files.

If your extracurricular activities include work in charitable, political, or civic organizations, as they should, you are going to meet search people somewhere along the line. (At Korn/Ferry, we encourage partners to perform that kind of work.) Search people are good people to make friends with. Even if you are at an early stage of your career, someday the acquaintanceship may lead to your being considered for a great opportunity.

And what about just sending in your résumé?

If you do so, you'll be in plentiful company. At Korn/Ferry, we receive literally thousands of unsolicited résumés every week. Some come from people who are merely unhappy, others, from those who fear they are about to be laid off. The résumés pour in from people at every level, from sales trainee to chief executive officer, and from every field. We once received a résumé from a fired college football coach. Unfortunately, it included his won–lost record, which was terrible.

Every incoming résumé is looked at in our research department, where most of them are put in a six-month-hold file. The best ones—from people we could be interested in if we had an appropriate search under way—are circulated (in summary) to our search partners and associates, and filed in our computer system. There they are coded by industry, type of job (finance, marketing, etc.), and position. Once in the computer, résumés are raw material for the future. Korn/Ferry and other large search firms are coming to rely more and more on their computerized data bases. Getting into those systems is a very important step.

If you mail off your résumé to a search firm and it is promptly tossed into the trash, you are at least no worse off than you were before. But there is a much better way to do it. If you are approaching the $75,000 salary level, you can just pick up the phone and call a leading search firm or two. Ask who specializes in your industry and leave word with his or her secretary that you are sending your résumé. Then, when it comes, it will go directly to a partner instead of a junior researcher. (In your résumé, do not neglect to state your current compensation. In a cover letter, indicate the kind of job you are interested in. If you are a senior vice president at a major company and are willing to move to a smaller company to get a higher position, say so.)

When your résumé is received, you may just get a thank-you note in return. But if your accomplishments are sufficiently impressive, you may be invited to a get-acquainted meeting, even though the search firm has nothing for you at the moment. Either way, a searcher will know you, and that can never hurt.

IF A HEADHUNTER CALLS

Then, someday, either through your own efforts to gain attention, or because your accomplishments have spoken for themselves, or because you just happen to be in the right kind of job in the right kind of company, a headhunter may telephone and say, "We are looking for somebody to fill such-and-such a position. Do you happen to know anybody?"

Receiving such a phone call should feel good. It is a compliment on what you have already achieved. But before you say yes, or no, or anything at all, get up and close your office door. If your office has no door, tell your caller you will get back to him. Conversations with head-hunters should be conducted in private. An inadvertently eavesdropping boss may be offended (or worse) that you are talking to such a person, even if you are about to say, No, thanks.

Once your privacy is established, listen to what the headhunter has to say. And tell him what he needs to know. There is no reason to be secretive, especially if you are not challenged where you are. Unless the job being offered is preposterously out of line, go meet with the headhunter. You have nothing to lose.

In the first interview, find out as much as you can about the job. Ask for the job description and for other informa-tion about the company. Study it, and then make up your mind quickly as to whether you are interested or not. If the job offers less opportunity than the one you already have, say, No, thank you. If you are interested, say so. Don't be coy. This is too important for game-playing.

In making your decision, keep in mind, as always, that while more money is attractive, money should never be the prime reason for making a move. The best reason for taking a new job, through a headhunter or anyone else, is to move up in growth opportunity and responsibilities (which eventually bring money). That is how major ca-reers are made.

PART 10

MONEY

FINALLY, LET'S talk about money. It may seem that the subject should have come up sooner. The desire to make money is, after all, one motive of every ambitious executive. But the topic of money, like money itself, is best approached indirectly. Successful careers result in large incomes. But the naked pursuit of a large income (as in changing jobs for a few dollars more) will not necessarily result in a successful career.

This is a lesson that needs to be learned by those just starting out. The 1960s hippie ethic is dead, and the business schools are packed with young men and women with materialistic values. Even Jerry Brown might agree today that "more is beautiful" (or, at least, that it is "pragmatic"). Up to a point, this is all good. Greed, made presentable as ambition, fuels the American economy, according to some.

But greed has a way of getting out of hand. The recent highly publicized insider-trading cases have involved a cohort of young Wall Street professionals whose careers promised success in every possible way. A little patience would have rewarded them with ample incomes. But greed led them to throw their promise away.

It is well worth noting that the senior managers in our survey—a seasoned group of successful, and well-paid, executives—when asked to choose the traits that enhance an individual's chances for success, named integrity above all others.

Most of Wall Street, like most of the general public, was appalled by the insider-trading scandals. The great bulk of American business is honest, for pragmatic as well as moral reasons. From two decades of experience as an executive recruiter, I can testify that it is considerably easier to place good people in a company whose reputation for honesty is intact than in a company tarred by the

Table 10–1

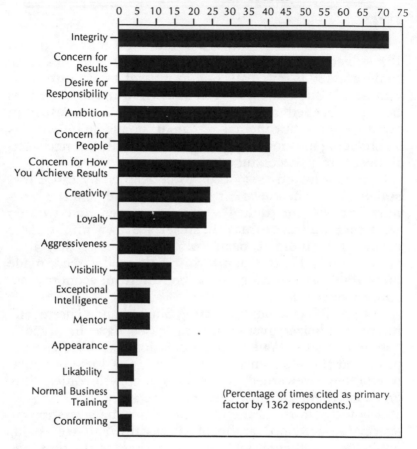

**TRAITS SAID TO HAVE GREATEST IMPORTANCE IN
ENHANCING AN EXECUTIVE'S CHANCES
FOR SUCCESS**

(Percentage of times cited as primary factor by 1362 respondents.)

malfeasance of one or more of its senior officers. Moreover, when a company has a major ethical lapse, its best people can be expected to start looking for ways to get out, no matter how well compensated they are or how content they may have been up to that point. All employees want to go home each night feeling good about the organization they work for. Give them reason to feel good, and they will reward their employer with increased productivity, longevity, and loyalty.

THE APPEAL OF MONEY

None of this is any reason to scorn money. Everybody wants money, and money can and should be amassed in large quantities during the course of an honest and successful career.

The desire to make money is, more often than not, the original motivating force for success. "My parents divorced when I was ten," recalls Ray Dempsey, chairman of the European American Bank. "My mother had to go to work. We lived in a four-room house with a coal furnace. We never had hot water in the house. When you go through that, if you get through that, you don't ever want to take a cold shower again. You don't ever want to eat cornflakes for supper."

"I wanted to be able to afford to do things that my family was not able to do," says Larry Horner, the chairman of Peat Marwick, "even though I might not have known precisely what they were."

All executives, from both poor and not-so-poor backgrounds, tend to be especially interested in money at the beginning of their careers. ("When you are flat broke, it is important," recalls Rockwell CEO Donald Beall. "When you start work in August and your first child is due in September, it is doubly important.") In the course of our interviews, I was struck again and again by how chief executive officers remember their first jobs' starting salaries, to the penny, thirty years after the fact.

Harry Gray remembers the starting salary of the first job he *didn't* take, that of assistant professor at the University of Illinois. "Assistant professors at that time were making thirty-six hundred dollars a year.... I had an idea I wanted to start at a higher salary."

Gray, who went on to a fabulous career at Litton Indus-

tries and United Technologies, was consistently motivated by money. "I started on that right after the end of
World War II," he recalls. "In some of those deep thoughts
that you have during a firefight or a place where your life
is in danger, you make yourself certain promises. I said, 'If
I live through this, I am going to achieve recognition for
myself and economic security.'"

After passing up the $3,600-a-year teaching job, Gray
went to work as a truck salesman. He did well, but he
soon moved on, because of what he saw as limited financial opportunity. "I was interested in finding a method to
participate in a business, not just work for a salary and a
bonus. The [truck] company I was working for wasn't interested in that....I went to Platt [Inc., as a bus salesman]
with the understanding that eventually I might be able to
buy a participation." By 1951, Gray was earning about
$14,000 a year selling buses. Then Korean War controls
mandated a cutback in the amount of steel allocated to
bus manufacturing. Gray suddenly confronted a massive
product shortage, and consequent loss of income.

He moved to Greyvan, a subsidiary of Greyhound,
where he rapidly rose to the post of executive vice president. At the age of thirty-four (in 1953), he was earning
$20,000 a year. But Gray was not to be satisfied earning a
salary plus a bonus. "I've always had a plan to try to find
some way to get some equity. I didn't inherit any money,
so I had to build something myself."

Gray saw a way to accomplish this when he picked up a
copy of Fortune magazine one day in 1952. "There was an
article about the new stock-option plans that the Congress had enabled through a piece of legislation, where
corporations could offer executives a discount on the
stock, and it could be as low as 25 percent of market
value. I went to the president of the Greyvan operation
and talked to him about putting in a plan of stock options
for our executives. Admittedly, I was included, but it was
fundamentally for the executive organization. He had
sympathy with it, but he said, 'This has got to be sold to
the parent company.' So he sent me over to a man by the

name of Orville Caesar, who was the chairman of the Greyhound Corporation. Orville Caesar was a brilliant automotive engineer who had designed these buses with the Greyhound and General Motors teams. His problem was he was not very, let's say, imaginative about motivating people, and the organization began to show signs of it. I tried for the better part of a year, before I gave up, to persuade him to put in a [stock-option] plan, not only for Greyvan but for the whole Greyhound organization." Caesar ultimately said no.

"There was no rancor, no great disappointment or anything. I told him, 'Well, I think what I ought to do then is find a company that would be interested in the kind of incentive program I believe in.' He said, 'I don't want you to leave Greyhound.' And he sent me to the West Coast, at his expense, to talk to a Mr. Ackerman who was running Pacific Greyhound and who subsequently became the head of all Greyhound. The idea was that Ackerman could convince me that I could make a lot of money working for Pacific Greyhound. I didn't take up with Ackerman, although I had great respect for the man, because, again, all he could offer me was salary and bonus, and I said, 'That gets taxed.' "

Gray began to look for a new job and heard about Litton Industries. He was initially attracted to Litton, where he was to make his major career breakthrough, because it offered the kind of compensation plan he had been seeking for years. "They had a stock-option plan, a very good one.... In the discussions I had with West Coast companies, the only one I found that was willing to really give you a chance on the stock options was Litton. I went from $20,000 a year [at Greyhound] down to $12,000 in order to get what turned out to be a large chunk of options. I had to take the risk with them." But that risk paid off handsomely. Litton prospered and Gray prospered with it, not only financially but also in stature and accomplishment. His pursuit of economic security put Gray on a path that led to his becoming one of the nation's leading corporate executives.

THE REWARDS OF THE TOP

Those who do reach the top of the corporate pyramid are awash in generous salaries and perks. Douglas McCorkindale, the vice chairman of Gannett, works in a handsome large office where his desk faces an entire wall of television sets. The day we met, he told us, "I have lunch being set up in my dining room next door. I have a bathroom here. I have a conference room back there. I have a kitchen. I could live here." So could a family of four. The average income (salary plus bonus) of the senior executives we surveyed is $235,000, and that figure does not include perquisites—or stock options.

"I can't begin to spend all the money I've made," Gary Wilson, executive vice president and chief financial officer of the Walt Disney Company, told us in our interview. "I created enormous wealth for myself [at Marriott, his previous employer] because all the things that I'd done for the prior five or six years were starting to come to fruition [when I left], so my stock options were starting to gain value.... I was able to cash out at very, very high stock prices... [and] I've got an enormous profit in Disney stock options."

Having a lot of money is great. I am a firm believer that rich is better than poor. But top executives, including Wilson, unanimously agree that money no longer has the allure it once held for them. "It's nice to know that you make a million or two million a year," Wilson says, "but that's not the reason we're in it.... I hire people to run my money, and I just write them checks. They run it, and I go about satisfying my ego needs in business."

Wilson has correctly named the game here. It is ego, not money, that drives the people at the top. Money is a major motivator early in corporate careers, but not later on. Once one's financial needs are met, once one knows that neither he nor his family will ever starve, then money plays a diminishing role in corporate ambition. Asked to define the components of success, senior executives rated money *sixth* on a list of seven elements.

Table 10–2

ELEMENTS NAMED AS MAJOR COMPONENTS
OF SUCCESS

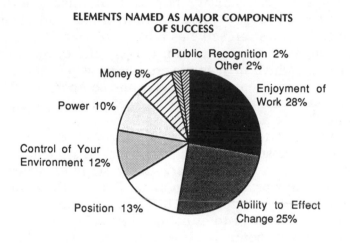

Public Recognition 2%
Other 2%
Money 8%
Enjoyment of Work 28%
Power 10%
Control of Your Environment 12%
Position 13%
Ability to Effect Change 25%

MONEY AS A SCORECARD

There is one purpose money always serves, however. It is a way of keeping score, from the beginning of one's career to the end. In this, it serves the ends of ego and also provides a practical yardstick for measuring one's progress at every stage of the road to the top.

As a freshly minted MBA from the University of Pittsburgh, Donald Beall went to work for Ford in 1961. "The thing that frosted me more than anything else," he recalls, "is that I started at five hundred dollars a month, and I found out that Harvard MBAs started at five fifty. That gave me an added incentive to pass the Harvard MBAs as fast as I could."

The motivating force provided by the desire to earn more than one's peers is an important one. Pay differences between peers are not haphazard. They matter. Nowhere is there such a direct connection between money and success as in business. There are titles, to be sure, but their value for comparative purposes diminishes across company and industry lines. Elegant offices and chauffeured limousines can serve as a basis for bragging rights but not for rigorous evaluation. Dollars and cents is the only way in which high achievers can measure their performance against that of their peers and competitors. The bottom line is the bottom line for people as well as organizations.

In low- and mid-level jobs, small salary differences are concrete manifestations of an employer's attitude toward its employees. A higher salary today signifies a better chance of being promoted tomorrow. Even at the highest corporate levels, where a difference of $50,000 might be only a few percent of total compensation, every distinction in salary or bonus is a message. Executives who no longer need the money still need to know how they rate in comparison with their peers, both inside and outside their own companies. "Money is not the issue," says Gary Wilson. "Money is the scorecard."

THE LESTER KORN AGE/WAGE RATIO

In my search experience, I have encountered a remarkable degree of ignorance on the question of compensation. Too often, executives are eager to consider offers from other companies just to find out what they are worth in the marketplace. They frequently have no idea what others earn in their industries, or even in their own companies. Without this comparative information, they literally do not know how they themselves are doing.

As a scorekeeping tool, the survey conducted by Korn/ Ferry International with the UCLA Graduate School of Management makes a unique contribution. We did not merely ask respondents how much money they *now* earn; we also asked what they *did* earn at every stage of their careers, from age twenty-five to the present. By adjusting their responses into 1987 dollars, we have been able to construct a lifetime age/wage yardstick of success. For the first time ever, up-and-coming executives can measure themselves against successful executives of an earlier generation and determine, objectively, how they are doing.

Here is a chart of the overall results, by age:

Table 10–3

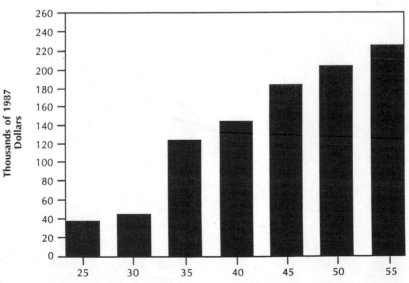

MEDIAN INCOME BY AGE

Depending on how you are doing at the moment, these numbers might strike you as high ($125,000 at age thirty-five!). But keep in mind that the people we surveyed have achieved senior vice presidencies at major corporations. We are dealing with high achievers here, not an average population. Those who eventually reach the top generally begin their careers by outperforming their peers, and that is reflected in their retrospective salary history.

As a general guideline, to keep up with this fast pack, you must earn 1½ times your age ($1,500 for every year) when you are twenty-five to thirty. After that, the multiplier increases. You must earn three times your age at thirty-five to forty, and four times your age thereafter. This is a far cry from the adage to simply "earn your age" that an older generation grew up on.

Table 10–4

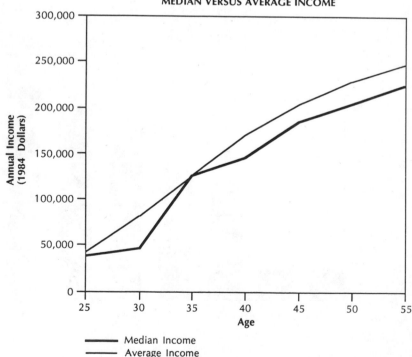

AGE/INCOME RELATIONSHIP
MEDIAN VERSUS AVERAGE INCOME

And even those ratios may not be good enough. The median income chart above tells only part of the income story of successful executives. Compare it with Table 10–4, which shows both median and average incomes.

Recall the difference between "median" and "average." A median is the point which divides a population in half. The median salary at age thirty is $45,549. That means half our respondents earned more than $45,549 at age thirty and half earned less. The average, on the other hand, we obtained by adding up all respondents' salaries and dividing by the number of respondents. The average salary at age thirty is $82,270, way above the median.

This tells us that a small number of successful executives increased their incomes dramatically between the ages of twenty-five and thirty, distancing themselves from their peer group. In fact, the top 25 percent reported incomes in excess of $144,000 at age thirty. This put them way above the bulk of the pack; 50 percent of their same-age peers were clustered between $25,000 and $45,549. This "top-heavy" situation pushes the average up sharply, while it has no effect on the median.

If only a small group made major salary breakthroughs before the age of thirty, a much larger number did so by age thirty-five. At that age, the median and average merge. There is no longer a significant advance column earning a great deal more than everybody else. By thirty-five, most executives headed to the top have made their major salary breakthroughs.

RATES OF INCREASE

Income rises at the fastest rate during successful executives' early years. Average annual gains decrease after the age of forty. (Of course, by age forty, successful executives are earning an average of $169,000. Even modest annual increases from that point on soon put their salaries into orbit.) Not only does the percentage increase diminish in later years; so does the actual dollar amount of raises. From ages twenty-five to forty, annual raises average

$8,508; thereafter they average $5,345. This shows, once again, that those who climb highest up the corporate ladder get off to a fast start. Those who fail to break out by the age of forty have little chance of breaking out thereafter, unless extraordinary efforts are made.

VARIATIONS BY INDUSTRY

The income picture painted so far is a composite of executives in all industries, and therefore may be somewhat misleading. Compensation does vary from industry to industry. In some fields, earning $60,000 at age thirty may mean you are doing just fine. In others (entertainment comes to mind), if you're making only $60,000 you are in big trouble.

The average current salaries of our respondents varied significantly by industry, with retail executives in first place and commercial bankers in last:

Table 10–5

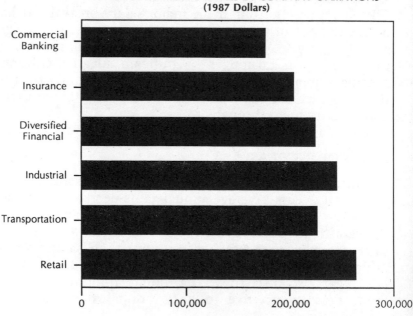

AVERAGE CURRENT SALARIES BY COMPANY OPERATIONS
(1987 Dollars)

Table 10–6

AGE/WAGE RATIO BY INDUSTRY

SALARY TRACK BY COMPANY OPERATION
(INCOME IN 1987 DOLLARS FOR EACH AGE)

	25	30	35	40	45	50	55
Commercial Banking	49,022	90,272	112,234	151,808	170,490	192,102	174,487
% Change	0	(84)	(24)	(35)	(12)	(13)	(−9)
Insurance	35,870	71,907	109,797	153,931	184,539	198,409	247,025
% Change	0	(100)	(53)	(40)	(20)	(8)	(24)
Diversified Financial	41,047	83,848	114,803	157,426	179,897	198,054	222,281
% Change	0	(104)	(37)	(37)	(14)	(10)	(12)
Industrial	38,947	79,369	129,566	176,351	215,968	241,235	256,704
% Change	0	(104)	(63)	(36)	(22)	(12)	(6)
Transportation	39,444	90,311	119,854	151,132	180,530	214,010	227,257
% Change	0	(129)	(33)	(26)	(19)	(19)	(6)
Retail	54,131	102,129	152,995	191,566	239,656	286,149	307,817
% Change	0	(89)	(50)	(25)	(25)	(19)	(8)
Overall	41,955	82,270	125,725	169,282	204,055	228,603	247,771
% Change	0	(96)	(53)	(35)	(21)	(12)	(8)

Table 10-7

EXECUTIVE COMPENSATION AND HOURS WORKED BY INDUSTRY
(1987 DOLLARS)

COMPANY OPERATIONS	MEAN SALARY	AVERAGE HOURS PER WEEK	HOURS PER DAY	DAYS WORKED*	TOTAL WORK HOURS	EFFECTIVE WAGE PER HOUR
Commercial Banking	$177,362	54.9	11.0	236.6	2,597.9	$ 68.27
Insurance	$205,827	54.1	10.8	236.2	2,555.7	$ 80.54
Diversified Financial	$225,534	55.5	11.1	237.8	2,639.6	$ 85.44
Industrial	$247,430	54.7	10.9	235.1	2,572.0	$ 96.20
Transportation	$228,818	53.4	10.7	237.8	2,539.7	$ 90.10
Retail	$264,948	52.6	10.5	236.6	2,489.0	$106.45
Overall	$235,387	54.5	10.9	236.5	2,577.9	$ 91.31

*252 workdays less number of vacation days taken

Interestingly, commercial bankers *begin* their careers earning more than anyone else but retail executives. Their salaries begin to fall behind those in other industries in their mid-thirties. Conversely, industrial executives (i.e., those in manufacturing industries) earn 7 percent less than the average executive at age twenty-five but eventually end up in second place.

Executives in all industries break the $100,000 barrier by age thirty-five. Retailing and industrial executives are the first to break the $200,000 barrier, at age forty-five.

Remarkably, in addition to earning the highest salaries, retail executives also work the fewest hours (an average of 52.6 a week, compared with an overall average of 54.5). All executives were asked how many hours they work each day and how many vacation days they take each year. (On average, they take 15.5 vacation days and work 54.5 hours a week). From these responses, we calculated the effective wage per hour of executives in every industry. Naturally, retail executives score highest, at $106.45 an hour. Commercial bankers (who work 54.9 hours a week) are lowest, at $68.27. Diversified financial executives, who take the fewest vacation days and work the most hours per day, earn $85.44 an hour. Overall, senior executives earn a comfortable $91.31 an hour.

VARIATIONS BY JOB

Despite the fact that only a few of our respondents named the international area as a fast-track career route (perhaps for fear of being away from the corporate power center), executives involved in international operations earn more, on the average, $286,420, than those in any other job specialty. General managers rank second, at $264,472; personnel executives, at $190,947, rank last.

International executives do not begin at high salaries; at age twenty-five, they earn less than most of their peers. By age thirty-five, they pull ahead to stay. Meanwhile, those in marketing and sales, who are ahead of their peers at age thirty, soon settle back into the pack.

Table 10–8

CURRENT SALARY BY JOB FUNCTION
1987 DOLLARS

FUNCTION	AVERAGE SALARY
International	$286,420
General Management	$264,472
Marketing/Sales	$249,109
Production/Manufacturing	$245,817
Finance/Accounting	$232,648
Personnel	$190,947

Looking at median as opposed to average salaries, we see that by age fifty-five, general managers are in a respectable second place. This confirms what we have long

Table 10–9

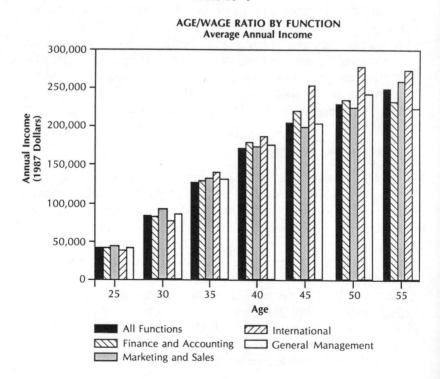

AGE/WAGE RATIO BY FUNCTION
Average Annual Income

Table 10–10

SALARY TRACK BY JOB FUNCTION IN WHICH MOST OF CAREER HAS BEEN SPENT
(MEDIAN INCOME IN 1987 DOLLARS)

	25	30	35	40	45	50	55
PROD/MFG	$36,837	$51,568	$120,142	$164,443	$185,138	$172,274	$225,191
INT'L	$36,516	$43,073	$136,596	$176,823	$215,758	$288,468	$293,857
GEN'L MGMT	$36,977	$44,292	$127,984	$152,829	$185,138	$202,185	$250,861
PROF/TECH	$36,516	$44,292	$117,010	$136,438	$170,236	$202,185	$203,596
MKTG/SALES	$38,006	$86,650	$135,576	$156,545	$185,138	$211,427	$245,511
PERSONNEL	$36,837	$44,012	$117,459	$128,348	$162,351	$168,736	$185,919
FIN/ACCTG	$39,423	$46,969	$125,105	$147,958	$194,268	$222,356	$221,348
OVERALL	$38,006	$45,549	$125,105	$144,418	$183,410	$203,596	$225,191

known from the volume and orientation of our search business: the majority of senior corporate executives are in general management. Few begin their careers there, but as they advance up the corporate ladder, the tendency is to assume more general responsibilities.

VARIATIONS BY JOB MOBILITY

I have already dispelled the myth that frequent job-hopping is the route to a high salary. Our survey shatters it. In every industry, executives who have had only one or two employers earn more than executives who have had three or more employers. In most industries, the salary differential is substantial.

Table 10–11

**CURRENT SALARIES BY COMPANY OPERATIONS
FOR LOW- AND HIGH-TURNOVER GROUPS**
1987 DOLLARS

	OVERALL	LOW	HIGH
Commercial Banking	$177,362	$187,215	$165,319
Insurance	$205,827	$226,629	$166,413
Diversified Financial	$225,534	$223,198	$218,965
Industrial	$247,430	$251,810	$243,051
Transportation	$228,818	$252,905	$205,827
Retail	$264,948	$283,560	$248,525

The picture of salary growth as related to job changing over time is more complicated. Initially, those who change jobs frequently are paid more than those who do not. At age twenty-five, high-turnover executives in every industry earn more than the average of their peers (19.8 percent more in retail, 8.9 percent more in commercial banking). However, by age forty, those in the low-turnover group surpass the job-changers in most industries. The only notable exception is in retailing, where the high-turnover group is ahead of the low-turnover group at age fifty-five.

Table 10–12

SALARY TRACK FOR LOW- AND HIGH-TURNOVER GROUPS

PERCENTAGE OF CHANGE FROM EACH
SECTOR'S AVERAGE

Age	25	30	35	40	45	50	55
Commercial Banking							
Low	(−7.0)	(−1.0)	2.6	2.3	5.5	5.7	0.9
High	8.9	2.0	(−3.0)	(−2.1)	(−7.7)	(−8.3)	(−1.0)
Insurance							
Low	(−4.7)	1.8	1.9	9.3	5.8	6.6	4.8
High	8.6	(−3.1)	(−3.4)	(−17.3)	(−12.5)	(−20.6)	(−18.5)
Diversified Financial							
Low	(−5.4)	(−10.0)	(−4.1)	(−0.3)	1.1	13.6	13.6
High	3.9	8.6	4.0	0.3	(−1.2)	(−10.0)	(−11.6)
Industrial							
Low	(−2.6)	(−1.7)	(1.2)	(−0.6)	5.3	3.2	5.5
High	2.4	3.1	1.7	1.3	(−4.0)	(−1.9)	(−6.4)
Transportation							
Low	(−3.4)	13.0	11.7	8.9	8.5	7.4	2.1
High	4.0	(−13.9)	(−12.8)	(−9.1)	(−9.0)	(−6.6)	(−2.1)
Retail							
Low	(−18.5)	10.5	4.8	4.4	(−8.1)	(−5.3)	(−9.9)
High	19.8	(−9.3)	(−4.5)	(−3.4)	8.1	5.6	13.5

YOUR JOB AND YOUR INCOME

What does all this mean to you?

Our survey results can tell you what you ought to be earning at every age, in every occupation, in every industry, to rank in the superstar class. If you find yourself lagging behind, do not despair. Get going.

One thing our survey makes clear above all else is that high salaries await those who perform well in the corporate world. It is no longer inconceivable for a relatively young manager to aspire to an income over $100,000 a year. There has been, across the board, a remarkable ratcheting up of salaries over the last decade. During the high-inflation years of the late 1970s, traditional annual merit increases of 4 to 6 percent were topped by substantial cost-of-living adjustments. Salaries leaped up. When inflation dipped, the psychology of large annual increases was hard to dislodge. At the same time, corporate competition for top performers has intensified. Between 1979 and 1985, the average incomes of senior executives surveyed by Korn/Ferry rose from $116,000 to $235,000. That is an increase of 103 percent, far outpacing inflation. A survey of chief executives by *Business Week* found that their average compensation had jumped up 18 percent (to $829,887) in 1986.

THE MYSTERY OF COMPENSATION RANGES

So high salaries are possible. They exist. And you might be in for a big surprise. Your own potential salary, *in your present job*, might be far higher than you imagine.

Most people assume, erroneously, that whatever they are being paid in their present position is the designated salary for that position. "I am an assistant vice president. I am paid $50,000 a year. Therefore, the designated salary for assistant vice presidents in this company is $50,000 a year."

Wrong. Most companies have formal compensation schemes, and those schemes establish not a single set figure but a *range* for each job. Those ranges are wider than most people realize. Typically, the top figure will be 50 percent higher than the bottom. Thus, a job like assistant vice president may be slotted at $50,000–75,000 a year. If you are earning $50,000, you may be at the bottom of the range and not know it.

Compensation bands have, if anything, been widening. To attract top talent, companies often have to pay newly hired people substantially more than they pay those they currently employ at the same level. When they do so, the compensation band for that job expands. Intense competition for star graduates of prestigious business and law schools has had the same effect. In recent years, some new graduates have been hired at starting salaries higher than the current salaries of star graduates hired two years before. As a result of premiums paid to new hires at all levels, compensation bands have in some cases actually begun to overlap. The range for assistant vice president may now be $50,000–80,000 while the range for vice president is $70,000–105,000. Some people are earning more than their bosses.

Clearly, it is in your interest to know the compensation range for your job. If you discover that you are at the bottom of the band, you may be able to negotiate a substantial raise without changing jobs or employers. If, on the other hand, you discover that your job pays $60,000–90,000, and you are already at $90,000, then you will know that you have exhausted that job's financial potential and can plan accordingly. (Knowing the range will also protect you from asking too little. Harold Geneen, who won fame and fortune at the helm of ITT, made this mistake when he was a job-hunting novice accountant in 1934, his biographer Robert Schoenberg reports. "At his interview with senior partner Norman J. Lenhart, Geneen asked for twenty dollars a week and was momentarily dismayed when Mr. Lenhart said, 'We can't pay that.' Geneen needed the job yet knew he could not get by on less. Mercifully, Mr. Lenhart went on, 'We'll start you out as an extra—at thirty dollars a week. That's our minimum.'")

You might be able to learn the compensation range for your job just by asking your boss. But your boss might not be willing to tell you. You might succeed in piecing it together by discovering the salaries of your youngest and newest peer and your oldest and most experienced peer. But such evidence can be trusted only if it is documentary. It's been my experience that most corporations will tell you salary ranges. They're not state secrets.

If all else fails, simply assume that your own salary is in the middle of a typical bottom-plus-50-percent compensation band. If you are earning $80,000, and you have been at your job for more than one year and less than five, it is not unreasonable to guess that you are near the midpoint of a $75,000–100,000 range.

NEGOTIATING YOUR SALARY

Now, how are you going to get your salary up to $100,000?

You are going to ask for it.

If your company has a merit review once a year in April, then January is the time to make your move. Do not wait until you have been given a 4-percent raise to let your boss know that you consider 4 percent inadequate. Let him know, before the deed is done, what you think is fair. Discuss your job performance with him. See if he agrees with you that you have done a fine job. If he does, ask, "Since I am doing such a splendid job, why am I getting only $80,000 when this job pays up to $125,000? If you are willing to pay 20 percent more to hire a new person, then why am I not worth 20 percent more?" Sometimes it is as simple as that.

Some of the senior executives we interviewed took pride in never having asked for a raise. "I never negotiated for salary," said James Harvey of Transamerica. "I was always given a salary or bonus as much or more than I expected."

"I have never asked for a pay increase in my entire life," said Ray Hay of LTV. "I have always believed that if you work harder and if you do a good job, people will see that you do it well, and you will be properly rewarded."

Darryl Hartley-Leonard, president of Hyatt Hotels, said that he too had never negotiated his salary. "In fact," he said, "I have been president for two months now, and I have no idea what my salary is. I have not asked. I did not ask at the time the job was given to me.... At some point I will say to [the chairman and the chief stockholder], 'How much shall I pay myself?' And they will say, 'X dollars.' And I will say, 'Okay.'"

These attitudes are fine for superstars, particularly those who entered business in an earlier era. Today it does not pay to be so passive.

James Harvey advises (despite his own history of never asking for money): "Just say, 'Look, I think I have done this wonderful job, and you may not be aware that I did a couple of these things.' Just lay it out.... Sometimes in the salary-review process your recommendation might have been made by a supervisor who didn't get along with you, and the people along the line might have thought you'd done a great job but nobody spoke up for you. So people should speak up for themselves."

Richard Braddock, sector executive of Citicorp, says he has done just that at the highest level. "John [Citicorp chairman John Reed] is a very open person, easy to talk to, and he basically deals with issues intellectually. The times that I have talked to him about [my compensation], I have attempted to create a frame that says not just 'Give me more money,' but 'Here is the way I think what is being done should be valued, and here are some of the comparative dimensions. Here is what So-and-So at American Express earns.' It is in that context." In that way, Braddock builds a case for himself.

In approaching your boss to discuss your pay, it helps to be confident. It helps to know the salary range for your job. It helps to have truly done excellent work. It helps to approach the subject gracefully. But the most important thing is just to do it, as Ray Dempsey, chairman of European American Bank, discovered many years ago:

"I started at Bankers Trust at eighty-five dollars a week. My first raise was eighteen months after that; I went from eighty-five to ninety. About a year later, I was given a second five-dollar raise. And I went to the head of the credit department, and I said, 'This is kind of insulting.'

He was a big guy, about six feet four, maybe 230 pounds, and he was almost shocked. I think it was probably the first time anybody ever got a raise and said it wasn't good enough. He said, 'You can't talk to me about that,' and sent me down to see my boss, who was under him. So I went to see the man, and I said, 'He told me to talk to you.' He didn't know what to do either.... About two months later, I was called in, and they said, 'We've re-evaluated your case. You are not going to get five dollars. You are going to get fifteen dollars.' So I went big. I went to a hundred and five. Because I complained."

BEYOND MONEY

When you are earning $90 a week, money is very, very important. But there comes a time in the career of every successful executive when the importance of money fades. The point at which this happens varies from individual to individual, but it happens to almost everyone. "At a certain stage *psychic* income is the major factor," says Darryl Hartley-Leonard, "and that stage comes when you are no longer worried about paying the rent."

This may be hard to accept when you are young and hungry, but there is an inescapable logic to it. Many top executives literally earn more money than they have time to spend. "It's a wonderful life in many ways," Evelyn Waldron, wife of Avon chairman Hicks Waldron, told *The New York Times* a couple of years ago. "We can afford to do all the things we like to do. But, on the other hand, we don't have the time to do all the things." Asked if he was a workaholic, former NBC chairman Grant Tinker denied it. "I don't kill myself [working]," he said. "But I don't do anything else."

Chief executive officers often drive themselves long

after the material rewards of doing so have lost their motivating force. "If I made a hundred thousand more or less, my lifestyle would not change at all," says Douglas McCorkindale. "I am not a big spender. I don't like to shop."

"The work is too hard to do it for a paycheck," says Ray Dempsey. "There's got to be a different drive to do the job. It isn't money." Our survey confirms the point: 70 percent of the respondents said they would continue in their present positions even if they were financially independent.

And yet, they certainly are driven to work. James Harvey, chairman of the Transamerica Corporation, has survived close bouts with cancer and a heart attack. After his heart attack, he recalls, "I was lying there looking at the ceiling and hearing the beeper beep. And that is a time you really re-examine your life.... You know very well that you're mortal and something could happen at any minute and you might die. And you really think that through pretty carefully. I basically decided that I really enjoyed what I was doing [at Transamerica] and that I would like to continue with what I was doing.... I had the alternative of lying on a beach in Hawaii or something." Harvey could have retired very comfortably. He chose to go back to work instead.

What is it about work that makes it so attractive to successful executives?

It involves ego, as I have said. It also involves fun. "I had always enjoyed going to work," Harold Geneen wrote in *Managing*. "In fact, I never thought of it as work. It was a part of my life, a part of the environment in which I lived and breathed. I often told colleagues that business was as much fun as golf, tennis, sailing, dancing, or almost anything else you might want to name. The pleasures were different from those of eating an ice cream sundae. Business provided intellectual challenges that stimulated and fed one's mind. They were every bit as good in their own way as the momentary pleasures of gobbling down one's dessert."

"You've got to have fun," concurs William Glavin, vice chairman of Xerox. "If you don't have fun in what you're doing, go do something else, because you spend too much time doing it not to enjoy it."

Top executives *do* have fun. (Eighty-six percent say that if they had it all to do over again they would pursue the same or a similar career.) Some love the sheer activity of their work. Darryl Hartley-Leonard has imagined that a small private hotel group might solicit his services. "Suppose they say, 'We will give you a piece of the action, and you will own a part of these three hotels, and after three years they will give you an income of five million dollars.' My response to that would be 'I would not take one more trip. I would not buy one more suit. I drive a nice car. I do not want a boat.' The biggest problem would be, if I had only three hotels, what would I do after eleven A.M.? What would I do with the time?"

Marshall Manley, chairman of Home Insurance, loves the sense of accomplishment he gets from building institutions. "I've always wanted to build," he says. "I've always built. In college I built up a fraternity that was small into the major fraternity on campus. The first law firm I went to was an eight-person firm. When I left there were over fifty lawyers. The next law firm was about a ten-person firm. When I left it was about sixty." Manley was next instrumental in building the law firm of Finley, Kumble, Wagner, Heine, Underberg, Manley & Casey into one of the largest in the nation. Now at Home Insurance, he says, "We are the seventeenth-largest property and casualty company in the United States. We're building and we're building. . . . When you stop growing, you start dying."

Other executives speak repeatedly of the exhilarating challenges of conquering circumstance and mastering new fields. "I'm interested in making something happen," says Norman Blake of Heller International. "My greatest thrill is to see some tangible result created through the people in this organization."

"I am certainly not working as hard as I am working

now to put more money in the bank," says William Waltrip, former president of IU International. "It is the challenge, the satisfaction I get out of a job."

There is an important lesson here for those who are
still on the way up. The things top executives love about
their jobs—the challenges, the learning experiences, the
opportunities to accomplish—are the same things they
sought in every job they ever had. In this their careers are
consistent wholes. The pursuit of the things they now
enjoy is what brought them to the top. As they climbed
the corporate ladder, they did not seek safe positions, or
positions with the highest salaries. They sought challenging opportunities, and those opportunities paid off for
them, as they do for the leaders of American business in
every generation.

And, I truly hope, so will the opportunities facing each
of you.

INDEX